香

# HONG KONG REVOLUTION

SPIRITUAL MESSAGES OF
THE GUARDIAN SPIRITS OF
XI JINPING AND AGNES CHOW TING

# RYUHO OKAWA

革 命

HS PRESS

# *Contents*

Preface .............................. 13

## INTRODUCTION

## Delving into the Tense Situation
## in Hong Kong

# CHAPTER ONE

# Spiritual Messages from
# the Guardian Spirit of Xi Jinping

## CHAPTER TWO

# Spiritual Messages from
# the Guardian Spirit of Agnes Chow Ting

CHAPTER THREE

# Spiritual Messages from Shiro Amakusa

CHAPTER FOUR

# Spiritual Messages from Hannah Arendt

# Afterword

# Preface

What is happening in Hong Kong—is it a protest or a riot? I would call it "Hong Kong Revolution". Hong Kong is now fighting a revolution against China's totalitarianism to achieve the foundation of freedom.

Hong Kong Chief Executive Carrie Lam announced yesterday the formal withdrawal of the extradition bill. This marks a partial victory, but the revolution would certainly not end.

This book clarifies the points of issue through the disputes of the guardian spirits of Mr. Xi Jinping and Ms. Agnes Chow.

It will help you deeply understand God's Will and the spiritual background of the conflict.

*Ryuho Okawa*
*Master & CEO of Happy Science Group*
*Founder and President of the Happiness Realization Party*
*September 5, 2019*

# Introduction

# Delving into the Tense Situation
# in Hong Kong

Recorded September 3, 2019
General Headquarters, Happy Science,
Japan

## *September 2019 is the critical time for the Hong Kong situation, ahead of China's 70th anniversary of its founding on October 1*

### RYUHO OKAWA

I've been concerned about the situation in Hong Kong with demonstrations going on for a while now. There has been a series of large-scale demonstrations, from one million to two million participants. The largest one yet was planned last weekend (August 31), but eight of the protest leaders were arrested on the day before. Ms. Agnes Chow was one of them. She was released on bail after being held in custody for several hours—less than a day. These series of arrests toned down the mood a bit, but the demonstration is still held on a voluntary basis. Since the beginning of September, students from universities, high schools and junior high schools have also been boycotting classes.

October 1 marks the 70th anniversary of the founding of China (the People's Republic of China), so the month of September will probably be the final critical time. Whether the demonstrators will give in to authorities as in the previous Umbrella Revolution*, or China will face humiliation, or it will end in tragedy—the ultimate outcome is unpredictable.

---

* A massive anti-government protest led by Hong Kong students in 2014 in response to China's growing political intervention to Hong Kong. The students participated in the protest while holding umbrellas, thus giving it the name "Umbrella Revolution."

The Japanese government will most probably remain in silence. If they were to complain to China, the number of Chinese shoppers in Japan will decrease. They might issue a statement to Hong Kong, but they are practically powerless. So, on behalf of Prime Minister Abe, who is visiting Russia, we, Happy Science, will speak for Japan.

## Getting in touch with the guardian spirits of Xi Jinping and Agnes Chow, the spiritual center of the Hong Kong demonstrations

### RYUHO OKAWA

There are many questions we want to ask today, but the core issues are the extent of President Xi Jinping's intentions and the opinions of Ms. Agnes Chow. While there are many demonstration leaders to obscure who really is in charge, in spiritual terms, I assume Ms. Agnes Chow is at the center. So, I would like to hear the opinions of her guardian spirit and see how far she intends to go.

China is aiming to seize Taiwan as well. Should they have trouble controlling the situation in Hong Kong or be humiliated now, it would make it difficult for them to make further progress to achieve their ambition. So, this will be a matter of how ruthless Beijing could be.

What is more, Hong Kong is now said to be the third biggest global financial hub, following New York and London, and it's a city with a trove of information. But under the current situation, it could possibly turn into a ghost town. Xi Jinping is now planning to move the financial hub from Hong Kong to Shenzhen on mainland China, so the fight will also be a battle for the very existence of Hong Kong.

## Seven million in Hong Kong confronting 1.4 billion in China, a totalitarian country in terms of international politics

RYUHO OKAWA

Analyzing China's political system in the context of international politics, almost everyone would agree that China is more of a totalitarian regime than a democratic system. And the question is whether the Hong Kong demonstrations will develop into a revolution or not. Out of the city's population of seven million, as many as one to two million people are participating in the demonstrations. Among the participants are family members of the police, and teaching and administrative staff of educational institutions. So this could truly be the final battle.

In terms of numbers, it's seven million people in Hong Kong against 1.4 billion people on mainland China, so if you do the math, you'll see that Hong Kong is out-numbered, 200 to 1. Hong Kong has no chance of winning if they were to fight China squarely. Therefore, for the demonstrators in Hong Kong, it all depends on whether or not they can successfully lead international opinion to turn against Beijing, forcing them to alter their policies toward Hong Kong before the situation turns into a tragic reality.

## Hong Kong is protesting to the promise-breaking Beijing, seeking to found freedom

### RYUHO OKAWA

Simply put, China broke its promise. After Hong Kong's return to China from British rule in 1997, China promised that it would allow Hong Kong to maintain its system for a period of 50 years. But although it has only been 22 years now, Beijing is already trying to incorporate Hong Kong into mainland China. Beijing is clearly violating the promise.

China broke its promise because they have a bigger ambition they want to achieve. They are trying to reach out to Taiwan, nearby Asian countries, Africa, and Europe. So, they can't wait so long. There are probably plans Xi Jinping wants to achieve while still in office.

If the definition of revolution is, as Hannah Arendt put it, "the foundation of freedom," then this is a rightful revolution. But if it leads to rule by fear, then the revolution would be a failure. At the present time, while there seem to be some radical aspects to the demonstrations in Hong Kong, my understanding is that, overall, they are seeking to found freedom. They seek freedom of expression and freedom of speech, as well as freedom to demonstrate and freedom to vote.

On the other hand, Carrie Lam, the current Chief Executive of Hong Kong, is probably a puppet of President Xi Jinping. I thought about recording a spiritual message from her guardian spirit, but she probably has no mind of her own. She can only do exactly as Beijing says, and she probably can't even step down on her own will. I don't think she can decide, not only whether to withdraw the extradition bill[*], but also whether to resign. So, I've decided to hear the opinions of someone who is "at the center" of the current situation.

## *Fighting a war of words to help support the desperate Hong Kong*

### RYUHO OKAWA

Happy Science has already published four books on Xi Jinping. They are: *Sekai Kotei wo Mezasu Otoko* (lit. "The Man Who Wants to be Emperor of the World") (Tokyo: IRH Press, 2010) and *China's Hidden Agenda: The Mastermind Behind the Anti-American and Anti-Japanese*

---

[*] On July 4, 2019, the day after this recording, Chief Executive of Hong Kong Carrie Lam announced the official withdrawal of the extradition bill which is the cause of the Hong Kong protests.

*Protests* (Tokyo: HS Press, 2012. See end section), and more recently, *Shugorei Interview: Xi Jinping Sekai Shihai e no Scenario* (lit. "Guardian Spirit Interview: Xi Jinping – Scenario for World Domination") (Tokyo: IRH Press, 2018) and *Xi Jinping Shugorei: Uyghur Dan'atsu wo Kataru* (lit. "Guardian Spirit of Xi Jinping: On the Suppression of the Uyghurs") (Tokyo: IRH Press, 2018).

From around last year, Happy Science has unveiled the reality of China's control over the Uyghurs and the dire situations in Tibet and Inner Mongolia and informed the world a lot. In March this year (2019), I also visited Taiwan[*] and posed a question if people in Taiwan want to see the same tragic future there. I'm sure my message has reached the people in China and Hong Kong as well.

We, Happy Science, too, want to do something to help the people in Hong Kong, but unfortunately, we still don't have political power. For now, all we can do is to exert an influence on society using the power of words.

Now, let us hear the true thoughts of Mr. Xi Jinping and Ms. Agnes Chow. On behalf of representatives from the media and governments around the world, we would like to ask questions to their guardian spirits and find out what they have to say.

---

[*] See *Love for the Future* (New York: IRH Press, 2019).

## *The Hong Kong people make their protests look like religious gatherings, as demonstrations are banned*

## RYUHO OKAWA

Typical demonstrations will get suppressed in Hong Kong now. So, to limit the extent of damage, demonstrators often make their protests look like religious gatherings. For example, they sing Christian hymns during their protests to minimize damage.

I heard that a Hong Kong demonstrator said, "If Jesus Christ were here now, he would most definitely not sit inside an air-conditioned house. He would surely be out in the streets helping people." Upon hearing this, I felt bad because my room is air-conditioned. But then, I thought perhaps it's fine because I'm not Jesus Christ. I just get down to what I can do.

At any rate, the situation is getting tense, so we can probably hear what they really want to say without spending too much time. Last week, we spoke with the guardian spirit of South Korean President Moon Jae-in and in it, he revealed his honest thoughts much more candidly than he did in the previous occasions. I have a feeling that today's spiritual interview will be similar.

The spiritual messages were channeled through Ryuho Okawa. However, please note that because of his high level of enlightenment, his way of receiving spiritual messages is fundamentally different from other psychic mediums who undergo trances and are completely taken over by the spirits they are channeling. Some spirits are able to use Master Okawa's language center and choose the necessary language to give spiritual messages, such as Japanese or English.

Each human soul is generally made up of six soul siblings, one of whom acts as the guardian spirit of the person living on earth. People living on earth are connected to their guardian spirits at the innermost subconscious level. They are a part of people's very souls and therefore exact reflections of their thoughts and philosophies.

It should be noted that these spiritual messages are opinions of the individual spirits and may contradict the ideas or teachings of the Happy Science Group.

# Chapter One

# Spiritual Messages from the Guardian Spirit of Xi Jinping

Recorded September 3, 2019
General Headquarters, Happy Science,
Japan

# Xi Jinping (1953 - Present)

Xi Jinping is a politician of the People's Republic of China. He is a member of the "Crown Prince Party"—a group of descendants of prominent Chinese Communist party leaders. In 2008, the National People's Congress elected him vice president of China. In 2012, Xi Jinping became chairman of the CPC Central Military Commission, which named him the successor of President Hu Jintao. In 2013, he was elected President of the People's Republic of China.

## Interviewers from Happy Science[*]:

### Jiro Ayaori
Managing Director
Director General of Magazine Editing Division
Chief Editor of *The Liberty*
Lecturer at Happy Science University

### Ryoko Shaku
Party Leader
Happiness Realization Party

### Motohisa Fujii
Associate Director
Special Assistant to Religious Affairs Headquarters
Director General of International Politics Division

*No statements made by the guardian spirit of Mr. Xi Jinping in this book reflect statements actually made by Mr. Xi himself.*

*The opinions of the spirit do not necessarily reflect those of Happy Science Group. For the mechanism behind spiritual messages, see end section.*

---

# 1

# Hong Kong and Taiwan are Facing the Imminent Danger of "Dominance of Fear"

## *Asking Xi Jinping's guardian spirit about his policy in the subconscious mind*

**RYUHO OKAWA**

Then, since we have a limited time, let's get started.

**JIRO AYAORI**

Yes, thank you very much.

**RYUHO OKAWA**

First, I will summon the guardian spirit of Chinese President Xi Jinping, who is on the side of oppression.

[*Takes a deep breath.*] The guardian spirit of Mr. Xi Jinping, the President of the People's Republic of China.

The guardian spirit of Mr. Xi Jinping, the President of the People's Republic of China. Please come down to Happy Science General Headquarters, and share your thoughts about the current Hong Kong protests.

The guardian spirit of President Xi Jinping. Please come down to Happy Science General Headquarters, and reveal your true intentions to us Japanese and people all over the world. Please. [*About 10 seconds of silence.*]

## *Referring to the time limits: "by October 1," and "before Taiwan's presidential election"*

**XI JINPING'S GUARDIAN SPIRIT**
Oh, hmm. Don't do this (publicly recording spiritual message) so many times. Hmm.

**AYAORI**
Thank you very much for coming to us at every crucial occasion.

**XI JINPING'S G.S.**
Stop bothering me.

**AYAORI**
Right now, all the eyes of the world are focused on Hong Kong, so we want to ask you for your opinion as the guardian spirit of President Xi Jinping to see how we should think about the matter.

**XI JINPING'S G.S.**
Well, I'm not involved anymore. It's the work of the lower staff, and Hong Kong's chief executive is responsible for that matter, so I have nothing to do with it.

**AYAORI**

I don't think the world's leaders and the media are looking at the situation in that way.

**XI JINPING'S G.S.**

So? Well, they are overestimating me. China is so large that I can't be bothered by everything that happens in it. All I said was, "Make sure all is 'cleansed' by October 1 (70th anniversary of the founding of PRC)." I can only give such a rough instruction, because I am the President of the People's Republic of China, you know?

**AYAORI**

Yes. That is a clear instruction.

**XI JINPING'S G.S.**

Hmm.

**AYAORI**

Now, here's leader (of the Happiness Realization Party) Ryoko Shaku, who just returned from Hong Kong.

**XI JINPING'S G.S.**

Huh? You went there? What were you doing there?

**RYOKO SHAKU**

I've observed the protest march on August 31 and a rally where people were singing a Christian hymn, "Sing Hallelujah to the Lord," and I can't but feel that the pressure by China is not working at all.

**XI JINPING'S G.S.**

Hmm.

**SHAKU**

The people of Hong Kong are all united, and I did not sense any fear from these people. What I felt from the people there was that they were all united or connected, focusing on their value of "protecting their freedom." I felt that this was having a significant impact on the world.

**XI JINPING'S G.S.**

Hmm.

**SHAKU**

How do you view the protests?

**XI JINPING'S G.S.**

I heard that about a thousand people were arrested, but the prison capacity is limited. There is a limit to the number of people that the Hong Kong police can put into custody, so the only other option is to take those arrested to mainland China. There, we have plenty of space to put them.

## SHAKU

Earlier, you said, "Make sure it is 'done' by October 1."

## XI JINPING'S G.S.

"Cleansed. "

## SHAKU

"Cleansed." Does that mean you have given an instruction?

## XI JINPING'S G.S.

Well, I guess you can say that. I'd like to have everything cleared by October 1, so we can have a parade in a happy mood.

## SHAKU

This year's National Day of the People's Republic of China will be the 70th anniversary of the founding of the country. In a sense, this is a day when China's dignity will be considerably on the line. However, Hong Kong Chief Executive Carrie Lam apparently said in a meeting with local entrepreneurs that she wasn't considering a time limit to end the demonstrations by October 1. But the central government thinks that October 1 is a breaking point, right?

**XI JINPING'S G.S.**

Wasn't spring of next year (2020) that thing in Taiwan? The presidential election?

**AYAORI**

There is one in January.

**XI JINPING'S G.S.**

Right? Next year, right? So, if we don't cleanse it before that, it will give influence over there, on Taiwan.

**AYAORI**

I think the Taiwanese will do their own...

**XI JINPING'S G.S.**

You know, if we show them what would happen if someone turned against China, then there will be a change in choice of the president of Taiwan.

**SHAKU**

Does that mean that you are shifting toward military intervention?

**XI JINPING'S G.S.**

Well, I don't know about all those minute details because I am in the position to manage all of China. The fact that they (the People's Liberation Army) have already gathered around Hong Kong indicates that the local officials can give the "go" sign.

**AYAORI**
I see.

**XI JINPING'S G.S.**
I don't know any of the details. I haven't given instructions on how many to dispatch, how many to capture, and how many to kill, or something like that. I may just say, "Suppress it."

### *"It might be better that Hong Kong Chief Executive would be shot dead than quit."*

**MOTOHISA FUJII**
According to today's news, Hong Kong Chief Executive Carrie Lam said at an informal meeting last week that she would quit if she could. This kind of news is now circulating. From this I have the impression that, in short, the regime side, or the Chinese Communist Party side, is no longer in solidarity and things are starting to get disorderly.

**XI JINPING'S G.S.**
Well, even she has to sleep like everyone else, so if she is

always the target of the demonstrators, of course she would feel that way. There really isn't anywhere to hide in Hong Kong. If there came as many as 1,000 protestors, there is no way to block them because they can climb anywhere. It's natural she would fear for herself.

**FUJII**

With respect to Taiwan, Mr. Xi Jinping announced, on January 2 of this year, the Chinese policy on Taiwan. Then, what happened was that, even though the support rate for President Tsai Ing-wen was not that high before, she rapidly gained support because the Taiwanese felt they had to work hard against China.

**XI JINPING'S G.S.**

This must be crushed. I need to crush it.

**FUJII**

In short, I feel that anything that Mr. Xi Jinping does turns out the opposite.

**XI JINPING'S G.S.**

Hmm.

**FUJII**

I think the international community sees it that way.

## XI JINPING'S G.S.

Well, from our point of view, they are only "a single ant." So, it's not that big of a problem. We really have to overcome the friction with other countries and spread "China's peace" throughout the world.

## FUJII

If Hong Kong were to be repressed, then it would probably work to generate a momentum in Taiwan to protect their freedom.

## XI JINPING'S G.S.

If Hong Kong Chief Executive Carrie Lam were to quit, I would rather have her be shot dead by a "fake police officer" disguising himself as a demonstrator.

## SHAKU

Did you say "a fake police officer"? It seems local people recognize that Hong Kong Police is now almost made up of military personnel, sent by the People's Liberation Army of the Chinese Communist Party. So, I guess it's true, then.

## XI JINPING'S G.S.

I think they are doing quite a lot of destructive activities, I mean, the police officers.

## Seventy thousand soldiers of the People's Liberation Army are already dispatched

### SHAKU

There already exist the People's Liberation Army camps in Hong Kong. There is a big building, I've seen it as well, and some people say that 70,000 soldiers of the People's Liberation Army are already stationed there, ready to move at a moment's notice.

### XI JINPING'S G.S.

Well, if the Hong Kong Chief Executive says she wants to quit. It's not good that she quits in a democratic way. It's better if she is shot dead by the demonstrators rather than her stepping down voluntarily.

### SHAKU

I see.

### XI JINPING'S G.S.

Then the international community will understand, even if the military officially intervenes.

### SHAKU

Are you thinking about staging something like that as well?

**XI JINPING'S G.S.**
Well, I can't deny any possibility of it. I mean, we never know what happens because there can be stray bullets everywhere.

**AYAORI**
There are also reports that despite Ms. Carrie Lam's suggestion of withdrawing the extradition law amendment bill, the Beijing government refused it.

**XI JINPING'S G.S.**
If she withdraws it, then she will be the one to be executed in mainland China.

**AYAORI**
Ah, I see. So, that is what you told her.

**XI JINPING'S G.S.**
Uh huh. So, maybe that is it.

**AYAORI**
I see.

**XI JINPING'S G.S.**
We would have no choice but to execute her. Or, she may die from an "illness."

## We will crush the protests, because they may spread to places like Xinjiang Uyghur

**AYAORI**
Umm. You said you were going to "cleanse by October 1." Demonstrations are now prohibited in Hong Kong and I think you will continue to do so in the future.

**XI JINPING'S G.S.**
Well, Japan would do the same. If around $1/200^{th}$ of Japan's population... how many will that be? Hmm? About 500,000?

**AYAORI**
Yes.

**XI JINPING'S G.S.**
Hmm. It is the same as about 500,000 citizens are going on a rampage saying they will become independent.

**AYAORI**
I don't think they are clearly saying "independence," but they do ask for "universal suffrage."

**XI JINPING'S G.S.**
Well, that's the same as independence.

**AYAORI**

Oh, so that is how you think.

**XI JINPING'S G.S.**

Yes, yes. If a sector is created that will not follow my command, then it is the same as that sector having become independent. You know, there is a risk that this may spread to Tibet, Xinjiang Uyghur, and Inner Mongolia Autonomous regions.

**AYAORI**

So, you are thinking about the whole picture.

**XI JINPING'S G.S.**

If we lose here, then it will spread to everywhere else, and may well be picked up by the foreign media, so we need to crush this quickly.

**AYAORI**

Even if you ban the demonstration, I think various protests will continue to occur sporadically even after that. Are you saying that you are going to suppress them by force?

**XI JINPING'S G.S.**

They have nowhere to run. That is their weakness.

**AYAORI**
Oh.

**XI JINPING'S G.S.**
They are at the tip of the peninsula, and the only choice left to them is to escape to the ocean, so they have to swim to escape. They can only jump into the sea, one after another, so they have no choice but to be shark bait.

**AYAORI**
I'm afraid Hong Kong would lose the function of a business location if it was suppressed that way.

**XI JINPING'S G.S.**
Actually, we have already considered that as well, and are intending to create a similar financial city in mainland China. This plan is already underway in the south, so it doesn't matter if Hong Kong is totally destroyed or becomes a ghost town.

**AYAORI**
That will have a direct impact on Taiwan, as you were concerned earlier, and people in Taiwan will come to think, "We can't deal with China anymore. We don't want to be swallowed by China."

## *"Fear is the ruler's best tool"*

### XI JINPING'S G.S.

That's not true. After all, as Mr. Machiavelli said, fear is the ruler's best tool.

### AYAORI

I guess you, yourself, are thinking like that, but...

### XI JINPING'S G.S.

There is no meaning in praising others, allowing freedom, or showing tolerance; "virtue" will not make people obey you. In the end, it is "fear" that matters.

### AYAORI

But rather, that fear will eventually lead to the Taiwanese people seeking freedom.

### XI JINPING'S G.S.

Even Taiwan has nowhere to escape [*laughs*]. I will show the world how much time it will take for us to suppress Hong Kong, so that Taiwan can see how little they can withstand against us.

### AYAORI

That will lead leaders from around the world, as well as the

Taiwanese, to think that China is not a country that can coexist with them.

## Next up: "Taiwan Province," the Philippines, Vietnam, and Thailand

### XI JINPING'S G.S.

No, that will not be the case. We will show how we deal with Hong Kong, and if that Taiwanese auntie with glasses (Ms. Tsai Ing-wen) becomes the president again, we will see how long it would take for us to "cleanse" Taiwan. Well, if we don't get Taiwan cleaned up, it will take time to control the South China Sea, the Philippines, Vietnam, and the surrounding area.

### AYAORI

What do you mean by "cleansing Taiwan"?

### XI JINPING'S G.S.

Huh? To make it "Taiwan Province" of course.

### AYAORI

Taiwan?

### XI JINPING'S G.S.

Taiwan Province of China.

**AYAORI**

Taiwan Province of China?

**XI JINPING'S G.S.**

Yes.

**AYAORI**

So, you are talking about annexation.

**XI JINPING'S G.S.**

Because the Philippines, Vietnam, and Thailand are naturally in our sight. That's the reason why we're building an airbase by reclaiming islands in the South China Sea, you know? Where do you think we will bomb from there?

**AYAORI**

At what point are you thinking of annexing Taiwan? Next January, they will have the presidential election, but will something decisive happen around that time?

**XI JINPING'S G.S.**

Because there is the Tokyo Olympics, it may be rather disgraceful for China not to be able to participate, so I must make necessary adjustments. But we would have to take Taiwan at least by around 2021.

**AYAORI**

So, you are planning to influence the election next year, and create a pro-Chinese...

**XI JINPING'S G.S.**

If the next president is pro-Chinese, then it wouldn't take more than two years for us to take over Taiwan completely.

**AYAORI**

In the case of a pro-Chinese president, you would make him agree to a merger to create Taiwan Province...

**XI JINPING'S G.S.**

Tourists would come from China, making the Taiwan economy rich, and Taiwan can also invest in China. It would be wonderful if we formed such a bond where neither of us could separate from one other, wouldn't it?

**AYAORI**

If a pro-Chinese candidate fails in the presidential election, would you use force, then?

**XI JINPING'S G.S.**

I probably will fire about 100,000 missiles (to Taiwan).

# 2

## Aiming to "Bring down" Trump in The 2020 U.S. Presidential Election

### *"Trump, who sold military arms to Taiwan, was frowned upon by the world"*

FUJII

I was thinking that the outcome of both Hong Kong and Taiwan issues will ultimately be determined by the U.S.-China relations.

XI JINPING'S G.S.

U.S.-China relations. Yes.

FUJII

Currently, the trade war is steadily progressing as President Trump originally said...

XI JINPING'S G.S.

He really is doing meaningless things.

FUJII

It is said that the Hong Kong demonstrations are substantially backed by American funds, and also linked to many other movements.

## XI JINPING'S G.S.

When Trump's negotiations with North Korea failed, I thought he would at least attack them, but he said something like, "I don't really want to do the U.S.-South Korea joint military exercises anymore. It costs money." So, I thought he was weak.

If he has trouble dealing with such a country like North Korea and says, "I don't really want to fight against North Korea because North Korea has atomic bombs and hydrogen bombs," then it means he has admitted that there is no way he can meddle with China. Should he trigger some clash in Hong Kong, it will cause a military confrontation with China.

Trump is hated by the world, so I think the harder he pushes the economic battle, the more isolated the United States will become. I feel like they will become an "orphan of the world."

## FUJII

The Trump administration has sold weapons to Taiwan, and shows the greatest support ever toward them.

## XI JINPING'S G.S.

That's why they are being frowned upon, right? Selling weapons at this time.

**AYAORI**
Only from China, that is.

**XI JINPING'S G.S.**
I don't think Obama, who loves world peace, would have done something like that.

**AYAORI**
I think the world accepts the U.S. selling of weapons to Taiwan, to some extent.

**XI JINPING'S G.S.**
Hmm.

**AYAORI**
Regarding the trade war between the U.S. and China mentioned earlier, I suppose it has inflicted a serious damage on China's economy with a negative growth rate...

**XI JINPING'S G.S.**
Well, that's all right. I mean, it's next year, right? The (U.S.) presidential election.

**AYAORI**
Yes, the presidential election is in November.

**XI JINPING'S G.S.**
Right now, we are setting up a lot of network to bring Trump down.

**AYAORI**
Oh?

**XI JINPING'S G.S.**
It's OK because we're working on it. We will take him down.

**AYAORI**
So, you think you can take him down?

**XI JINPING'S G.S.**
Yes, we will take him down.

**SHAKU**
What do you mean by "taking him down"?

**XI JINPING'S G.S.**
We will change it to a Democratic administration. We have such power.

**SHAKU**
In particular?

**AYAORI**

Do you mean you will intervene in the election?

**XI JINPING'S G.S.**

Of course. We are pouring money into the anti-Trump camp, and also taking action.

**AYAORI**

Some media are also under your influence, aren't they?

## *"We replaced the mayor of Kaohsiung in Taiwan"*

**XI JINPING'S G.S.**

It's not just Taiwan. Well, we are intervening in Taiwan, too.

**AYAORI**

Yes.

**XI JINPING'S G.S.**

We replaced the mayor of Kaohsiung. We will do it in the U.S., too. China's power is already that great.

**AYAORI**

I see. On the other hand, China's economy was rattled by the trade war and marked negative growth, and it has now come to a point where the yuan might plunge. Furthermore, there are signs of inflation, and it seems that the Chinese Communist Party has lost the support of the citizens to a dangerous level. In this sense, you are being pushed into a tight spot, is that correct?

## XI JINPING'S G.S.

No, that's not true. I think the U.S. will be isolated from the world before long, and will declare that they will no longer interfere with any conflict in the world. They will probably do something like the "Monroe Doctrine"* again.

## AYAORI

I think the U.S. will keep the same policy against China.

## XI JINPING'S G.S.

But Trump's time is soon coming to an end. So, even if he continues with his policy, it is only for a bit longer. We just need to hold out for another year.

## FUJII

But the fact is, in the prospects for the U.S. presidential election, the Democratic Party does not have particularly

---

* A foreign policy statement made in 1823 by the 5th president of the United States of America, James Monroe. It was a statement to separate spheres of European and American influence.

strong candidates. Plus, the Trump administration's economic policy has been working well, and it is being said that Trump has an overwhelming advantage, without many drawbacks.

## XI JINPING'S G.S.
His policy may have been good a little, but after having started the economic war or the trade war with China, the U.S. growth rate is now declining rapidly. We may be in a bit of a slump, but still, we are at six percent or so.

## AYAORI
That is a bit suspicious.

## XI JINPING'S G.S.
On the other hand, the U.S. growth rate is now going to decline to one percent or so. It is dangerous, indeed.

## FUJII
But isn't there much more damage to China than there is to the U.S.? Recently, there was a suspicion of China trying to manipulate the yuan to be weaker, but this seems like a dangerous sign of yours.

## XI JINPING'S G.S.
I hear that the number of tourists going to Japan from

South Korea is decreasing now, and the Japanese inns seem to be in deep trouble, but I think the Japanese economy will cool down if the Chinese tourists stop visiting.

## AYAORI

I think Japanese people have to keep moving forward with those risks in mind. However, in regard to the trade war between the U.S. and China, President Xi, himself, is saying that China must be ready to fight a drawn-out war, that they have to endure it. He is saying such things in his speeches in multiple places.

## *What does he really think about the trade war?*

## XI JINPING'S G.S.

I'm just saying it in a bit harsh way. We will overtake the American economy in the next few years. We just really have to endure until then. We just have to do well until then but they suddenly are taking an aggressive stance.

## AYAORI

The point is, as long as Mr. Trump is in charge, things will be hard for you.

## XI JINPING'S G.S.

But there is the possibility that Trump will be ousted by his people.

**AYAORI**
Well, yes, there is that possibility.

**XI JINPING'S G.S.**
Yes.

**AYAORI**
So, I guess what you are saying is that you want to survive the Trump administration somehow, that you need to endure.

**XI JINPING'S G.S.**
American intellectuals are anti-Trump.

**AYAORI**
Well, that is true.

**XI JINPING'S G.S.**
Nothing that bears the name of Trump will sell. So, as far as the future is concerned, the writing is on the wall. Even if the U.S. imposes a tariff on Chinese products, it is the American buyers, or the customers, who are losing because they eventually have to buy those at a higher price. The Americans are starting to realize that they are losing out.

After all, they are just being forced to buy something expensive, and the Americans are starting to realize that it is the same as a tax increase, so he won't last for long.

## SHAKU

In China, too, the tariff war with the U.S. raised food prices and it hit the common people's kitchen. So, their dissatisfaction with the government is growing quite a lot. In the case of the Tiananmen incident, too, it is said that the democratization movement occurred because people were dissatisfied with the steep rise in prices, resulting in their inability to buy pork. Even so, do you think there are no problems within your own country?

## XI JINPING'S G.S.

There are no "common people" in China. The Chinese are all like civil servants, and there are no commoners. We are different from your country.

# 3

# Extremely Outdated Sense of Politics and Human Rights

## *"We will spread 'Chinese-style democracy' throughout the world"*

### AYAORI

I'd like to go back to a previous topic. In regard to Hong Kong, you arrested participants and democratic leaders at last Friday's (August 30) demonstration.

### XI JINPING'S G.S.

Yes.

### AYAORI

Those arrested included Ms. Agnes Chow and Mr. Joshua Wong, among others. I'm wondering, did you order the arrests?

### XI JINPING'S G.S.

No, I had nothing to do with it. But letting them out on bail in less than a day is pretty spineless. And it was cowardly of them to pay the bail, too. They still claimed that they were going to hold the biggest demonstration ever on the day after that, but it turned out to be a small, scattered rally. It looked very weak to me.

**SHAKU**

It wasn't small or scattered at all.

**XI JINPING'S G.S.**

Yes, it was.

**SHAKU**

I beg to differ. It was not small or scattered.

**XI JINPING'S G.S.**

They had hoped to gather more than two million people, but once we arrested the two main figures they quickly got weak in the knees.

**SHAKU**

I'm afraid your understanding of the situation is quite far from the reality.

**XI JINPING'S G.S.**

That kind of thing doesn't get news coverage inside China. So, I don't really know.

**SHAKU**

The streets of Hong Kong were endlessly so full of people participating in the demonstration, which made me wonder where they were all coming from.

**XI JINPING'S G.S.**
Well, it's a small place.

**SHAKU**
Everyone from adults to children, including school teachers and students in junior high school and high school, all stood and took action. The whole world watched it intently and is now starting to realize the pressure being applied by China's Communist Party. I can't help but get the feeling that you are asleep at the wheel.

**XI JINPING'S G.S.**
The Communist Party of China is the "standard-bearer of democracy." We are at the center of the world. And we are just trying to spread Chinese-style democracy throughout the world.

**SHAKU**
And what kind of democracy is that?

**XI JINPING'S G.S.**
Well, as you can see, we are trying to do away with the world in which crafty people, like the Americans, are making money hand over fist, and instead create the one where everyone prosper purely, properly, and equally.

AYAORI

There is no equality in China, though, right?

XI JINPING'S G.S.

It most certainly is.

AYAORI

It's a country with one of the largest wealth disparities.

XI JINPING'S G.S.

No, no, no. That's just someone's intentional propaganda.

## *"We will round up the younger generation and send them to the Xinjiang Uyghur region"*

SHAKU

The younger generation in particular (in Hong Kong) no longer fear China's Communist Party at all.

XI JINPING'S G.S.

I've never heard of that. That's not true.

SHAKU

Joshua Wong, Agnes Chow, and others have formed a new political party called Demosisto. The way the younger generation there thinks is completely different from how the Japanese think. They haven't been brainwashed by China. Do you have anything you want to say to the younger generation?

**XI JINPING'S G.S.**
Well, we will have no choice but to round them all up. It's like the old saying, "Out of sight, out of mind." If we round them all up and put them out of sight, then that will be the end.

**SHAKU**
Do you not realize how much the people around the world despise such way of thinking?

**XI JINPING'S G.S.**
If we just nab them and send them to Xinjiang Uyghur, then that would be the end. Among other Uyghurs, they wouldn't be recognized.

**SHAKU**
But the Uyghur people are already a focus of the world's attention.

**XI JINPING'S G.S.**
There are currently as many as two million people (in the concentration camps in Xinjiang Uyghur), so it would work out. If we were to put them in there, no one would ever know.

## AYAORI

From the objective, global view, Hong Kong itself is already considered anti-regime against the Chinese Communist Party regime.

## XI JINPING'S G.S.

Hmm. Then they are currently being tested to see if they are willing to go as far as to start a revolution. They have no hope of overthrowing mainland China with just demonstrations. It's not possible. Besides, we have already outlawed demonstrations.

## SHAKU

Peaceful demonstrations for democracy are no longer allowed. But there are still various activities going on and...

## XI JINPING'S G.S.

Their only option is a revolution. And if they want to start a revolution, they will need weapons. But it's the police and military who have the weapons. The demonstrators do not have any.

**"The 'rats' attempting democratization should get out! Then, there would be peace."**

## SHAKU

People indeed have no arms.

**XI JINPING'S G.S.**
Right, so we can wipe them out.

**SHAKU**
Maybe so. They do appear woefully powerless. However, in a sense, those unarmed demonstrators also seem to be igniting the flames of revolution around the world.

**XI JINPING'S G.S.**
No, they are just screaming for help. They just say, "Help us!" So, they're not very brave. They should just hurry to death without calling for help.

**SHAKU**
But in reality, the U.S. Congress has clearly started to show their support to Hong Kong. And the same move is underway in the U.K., too. Up until 1997, the year England handed over Hong Kong, citizens of Hong Kong were allowed to hold a British passport while ethnically being Chinese. They had such a system and now, the U.K. is considering providing the citizens of Hong Kong with full British citizenship. In this way, the whole world is now acting to help Hong Kong.

**XI JINPING'S G.S.**
No, they are just worried that many immigrants will be produced from Hong Kong. But that's fine. They should

just leave. Japan should accept some of those immigrants, too. I wish all the troublemakers would run away. Then, we will be able to create a "peaceful," commercial city. That would be better. I hope a million of them would run away. They should emigrate somewhere. We have enough people to cover for them. If they leave, we will just allow influx of the mass of people from somewhere in China.

## AYAORI

What you are talking about right now implies exactly that the second Tiananmen Square incident will happen in Hong Kong.

## XI JINPING'S G.S.

No, it might not happen. Not if all the "rats" leave first. Hong Kong is along the coastline, so they will drown to death, should they jump in. They will have no choice but to run away.

## AYAORI

I think that is what would happen if you were to use military force. But if you did, countries around the world would begin to impose sanctions, just like they did after the Tiananmen Square incident.

## XI JINPING'S G.S.

We got through that, though, didn't we? We aren't as clumsy as Russia.

**AYAORI**

It was Japan's mistake to have supported China at that time.

**XI JINPING'S G.S.**

We successfully overcame it.

**AYAORI**

So, you are saying that it will happen again, right? And, this time...

**XI JINPING'S G.S.**

You know, the Tiananmen incident only had between 2,000 to 10,000 victims at most, even according to high-end estimates. There is no reason for you to bring up such a small incident after decades have passed.

**AYAORI**

You're saying that the same thing could happen in Hong Kong too, right?

**XI JINPING'S G.S.**

In Hong Kong, the same number of people would die in a matter of one day.

## "There is no need to give the citizens freedom because they are all civil servants"

**FUJII**

President Trump is actually calling for a humanitarian solution in order to prevent a second Tiananmen Square incident.

**XI JINPING'S G.S.**

Even so, if Trump is brave enough to dispatch an aircraft carrier off the coast of Hong Kong, let him try. He's a businessman, so the only thing on his mind is business. And when push comes to shove, he is completely incompetent. If he thinks he can do it, let him try.

**FUJII**

But actually, suppression through military force would be...

**XI JINPING'S G.S.**

Send an aircraft carrier. I dare him. We have developed missiles that can penetrate the deck of an aircraft carrier, so if he does, we will fire a missile onto it. And it would be in self-defense. It would be completely natural for us to attack if our sovereignty were threatened.

We are not like Japan at all. When six members of the South Korean National Assembly stood on Takeshima Island, cheering and waving a Korean flag around, Japan was unable to do anything but just say, "It's regrettable." If the island had belonged to China, we would have blasted it with missiles, one after another, if Korea had sent in six National Assembly members like that. That's the kind of country we are. We are different from you.

## SHAKU

But there is actually a difference between now and at the time of the Tiananmen Square incident, where young people who had never known freedom rose up and got quashed. In Hong Kong, people who grew up breathing the air of freedom are about to be suppressed. The situation is totally different, don't you agree?

## XI JINPING'S G.S.

That Tiananmen incident was tenaciously and annoyingly dragged on for months. It should have been over quickly. The government must have been patient with it at the time. And even some government officials were trying to stand up for the students. The government had to oust them before it brought an end to the incident all at once.

But now, in Hong Kong, there is no one in the Chinese government who is trying to speak up for them. My complete autocracy has already begun. No officials of the Chinese Communist Party can defy me. Who was that guy...?

**SHAKU**
Hu Yaobang and Zhao Ziyang?

**XI JINPING'S G.S.**
Yes, Hu Yaobang (and Zhao Ziyang). At the time of the Tiananmen Square incident, they were trying to protect the students. But Zhao Ziyang fell from power because of it. The entire incident was put to an end after dismissing him.

**SHAKU**
So, he was forcibly stripped of power, then?

**XI JINPING'S G.S.**
Yes. But now, there is no one I should dismiss. There is no one left who doesn't do what I say.

**AYAORI**
I imagine people are now talking behind your back in hushed tones every day.

**XI JINPING'S G.S.**
Ah, no. There's no way they could.

**AYAORI**
But among the members of the Communist Party, there are also those who believe in democracy.

## XI JINPING'S G.S.

If someone in Zhongnanhai (the central headquarters of the Communist Party of China) were to express the desire to protect the people in Hong Kong, that might motivate the demonstrators a lot. They may then hope that the Beijing government might change as they continue their protests, but there is absolutely no possibility of that happening.

## SHAKU

Since 1997, there have been quite a lot of emigrants from China to Hong Kong. And among those Chinese immigrants, an increasing number of people are joining the Hong Kong demonstrations because they have tasted freedom themselves.

## XI JINPING'S G.S.

Ah, that's not a problem. We could send in tens of millions anytime. We have plenty of people.

## SHAKU

I get the feeling that you take freedom and democracy too lightly.

## XI JINPING'S G.S.

There is no need to give people this so-called "freedom." Civil servants don't have freedom. And all Chinese citizens are national civil servants. They don't have freedom. They have no choice but to act under the law. If the law forbids something—in the way that it forbids demonstrations—then they have to do what the law says.

## *A plan to form a major financial and trading metropolis by combining cities such as Hong Kong and Shenzhen*

### AYAORI

You might be able to suppress Hong Kong that way, but I think what is happening right now is a wonderful thing. People can now go from Shanghai or Beijing all the way to Hong Kong by high-speed railway, right? A lot of people from mainland China go there as tourists, to see the ongoing demonstrations with their own eyes. Some of them even participate. In that sense, we can say that an anti-Xi Jinping sentiment is growing in Hong Kong and an increasing number of people from mainland China are witnessing this and joining the protests. Is that right?

### XI JINPING'S G.S.

No, no. You have very narrow vision. What I am proposing is a larger financial city, beyond just Hong Kong. I have announced a major proposal to create a huge financial city and an international trading city in southern China by combining Shenzhen, Macao, and other places, including Hong Kong. To do that, those people who are only concerned about such "tiny gatherings" of Hong Kong need to be removed. We need to replace them with others, because they don't seem to understand my idea.

## AYAORI
But now China is already losing capital. Fewer investments are being made in China, so I suppose a financial city like that wouldn't function.

## XI JINPING'S G.S.
Hmm. Whatever. About the emigrants, the only places they could go would be England, the U.S., Taiwan, or Japan. That's it. If they want to go, then I hope those "rats" all run away. Anyways, we need to replace them to make things work properly, so I'm not worried about it.

## SHAKU
You keep mentioning "replacing" them, but Hong Kong is the window for investments into China. So, if the People's Liberation Army were to enter Hong Kong, foreign investments from the U.S., Japan, and other countries would naturally dry up. And companies in Hong Kong would gradually start making their way out. It would be just like killing the goose that lays the golden egg.

## XI JINPING'S G.S.
Well, that may be unavoidable. That's why we will make sure to transfer those functions to Shenzhen.

**SHAKU**

But Shenzhen and Macao are completely different from Hong Kong. Don't you think?

**XI JINPING'S G.S.**

We intend to make them develop into even more advanced cities than Hong Kong. They will serve as a replacement, so there is no problem. We are going to make sure that people can invest overseas directly from southern China, instead of from Hong Kong, and we will also attract investments there. We must not just let the opinion of 1/200th of our population (the citizens of Hong Kong) dictate the future of the other 199/200th (mainland China). That would be misunderstanding the main focus and the trifles.

## The subconscious of Xi Jinping significantly misjudges the U.S. power

**FUJII**

You say Hong Kong has just 1/200th of your population, but you have to consider the trade tariff issue with the U.S. If you make a mistake in how you deal with Hong Kong, it could cause huge problems. Even now, China looks quite driven into a corner. But what is the actual situation?

**XI JINPING'S G.S.**

It's not affecting us at all. [*Laughs.*] The U.S. is an

agricultural nation. Most of what they demand China to buy is agricultural produce. And they are upset over our imposing tariffs on that. They just tell us to buy soybeans and other agricultural produce, so the U.S. is, after all, an agricultural nation. From the viewpoint of China, it truly is an underdeveloped country.

**FUJII**
Their capitalist economy is functioning, though.

**XI JINPING'S G.S.**
What do you know? Most of their industrial sector is out of business. They are rusting. They even have a region called the "rust belt."

**SHAKU**
Umm, you are probably...

**XI JINPING'S G.S.**
What?

**SHAKU**
I can't help but think you're joking...

**XI JINPING'S G.S.**
Hmm. They lost all of their automobile factories after losing out to Toyota. The country is full of unemployed people.

**SHAKU**

Are you serious? What you are saying is making me worried.

**XI JINPING'S G.S.**

The one thing the U.S. can be proud of is their large-scale farming. That's it.

**AYAORI**

You say that because you stayed on a farm like that when you were studying abroad there, is that right?

**XI JINPING'S G.S.**

Well, I saw the central part of the U.S. when I was studying there. It was amazing. They would spread disinfectant from the sky using propeller planes. Their farms are truly huge. That's quite an amazing scale.

**AYAORI**

You probably think like that because all you saw was the countryside.

**XI JINPING'S G.S.**

As an agricultural nation, they are indeed advanced. In China, it wouldn't be worth spending money on the helicopter.

## SHAKU
[*Gasps.*]

## FUJII
No, no. As we can see from the case where President Trump recently designated China as a currency manipulator, China is the one that seems to be more of a primitive country from the viewpoint of international society.

## XI JINPING'S G.S.
Trump is a real estate developer, isn't he? How would a real estate developer know anything about currency exchange? Incidentally, most of what China engages in is construction as well. All we do now is constructing buildings.

## FUJII
Well, I think the actual reason you are in such a dangerous position now is because Chinese leaders don't understand economics.

## SHAKU
That's right.

## XI JINPING'S G.S.
We are not in any danger.

**SHAKU**

Buildings constructed by real estate developers in China are all defaulting on their loans.

**XI JINPING'S G.S.**

Well, if Trump has the guts, I dare him to build a Trump Tower in China. We would be able to immediately seize it. China is a "powerful" country like that.

**SHAKU**

[*Smiles wryly.*] I'm afraid you don't seem to understand that it will exactly have the opposite effect on economic prosperity.

**XI JINPING'S G.S.**

You know, countries like them are in the wrong. I don't know anything about the Republican or Democratic parties, but once the Democrats take over the administration, they really should just seize the Trump Tower and add it to their national treasury.

### Facing the first decline in tax revenue in 51 years and an aging society: "We'll just dig holes and bury people"

**SHAKU**

I get the feeling that what you are saying sounds like a comedy a bit.

**XI JINPING'S G.S.**

What's so funny about it? This is the proper way of thinking. What are you talking about?

**SHAKU**

I think it's "over" now.

**XI JINPING'S G.S.**

It's not over. It's just beginning. What are you talking about? The whole world is starting to undergo "Chinalization."

**SHAKU**

Oh, my... [*Gasps.*]

**XI JINPING'S G.S.**

The world will be coming under the influence of China... All of Asia will "Chinalize," and even Africa will "Chinalize."

**FUJII**

I think anyone who hears this conversation would probably think that President Trump is a cut above you.

**XI JINPING'S G.S.**

Really? I wonder.

**FUJII**

People would say that China is the one being driven into a corner.

**XI JINPING'S G.S.**

Mr. Trump is now more and more on the retreat.

**SHAKU**

Such a view just shows that you don't understand anything. President Trump is smart and...

**XI JINPING'S G.S.**

But the U.S. is pulling out of South Korea and pulling out of Japan, and now they are even trying to turn China, their biggest trading partner, into an enemy. They are on the verge of self-destruction.

**SHAKU**

What about China? It just experienced the first decline in tax revenue in 51 years. What is more, the average age in China is expected to rise significantly. Are you sure your country will have no problem domestically?

**XI JINPING'S G.S.**

Ah, we have no problem. In China, we can just dig holes and bury people. It won't be an issue. We are not like Japan. We cannot afford to keep those "money-mooching" old people around like pets, like you do in Japan.

## *"Human rights are an example of mistaken Western thought. They don't actually exist."*

**SHAKU**

No matter where you go in the world, people talk about human rights...

**XI JINPING'S G.S.**

No such thing exists.

**SHAKU**

But even China is beginning to wake up to the idea of human rights.

**XI JINPING'S G.S.**

The president is the only one who has any real authority.

**SHAKU**

No, for example, there was a major earthquake in Sichuan, and...

**XI JINPING'S G.S.**

Who cares? Who cares if they die? It lowers the population.

**SHAKU**

The earthquake destroyed a poorly-constructed elementary

school, and that caused quite a lot of people to wake up to the idea of human rights, even within China.

## XI JINPING'S G.S.

Ah, that's just an example of mistaken Western thought. It needs to be eradicated.

## SHAKU

I'm afraid you may be lacking in intelligence if you don't see how dangerous that line of thinking is.

## XI JINPING'S G.S.

What are you talking about? According to America's "wanna-be" egalitarians, they say that "All men are created equal," but that is a lie. That does not comport with reality at all. The president of China and the "rats" in Hong Kong are in no way equal. I am completely different from them.

## SHAKU

I am starting to doubt your intelligence; maybe you are fatally lacking in it.

## XI JINPING'S G.S.

No, I'm highly intelligent. What are you talking about? Do any of you have any idea what it's like to be an "emperor" ruling over 1.4 billion people?

**SHAKU**

[*Gasps.*]

**XI JINPING'S G.S.**

Well? Would an ant be able to understand how it feels to be God? Huh?

**SHAKU**

Do you know the Will of God?

**XI JINPING'S G.S.**

I am a god, so yes, I do know it.

**SHAKU**

Ah.

**XI JINPING'S G.S.**

I am sure God thinks the same way I do.

**SHAKU**

God would see a person with such an idea as an ant.

**XI JINPING'S G.S.**

I rule over 1.4 billion people, and now I am in the process of expanding this control to over 7 billion people in the world. And the EU will be under China's influence very shortly.

# 4
## "The Country of Japan will Disappear"

### *A fundamentally mistaken view of how far the Chinese economy has fallen*

**SHAKU**

I'm going to change the subject a bit. I would like to ask you about Japan. On December 24 this year, Prime Minister Abe will go to China for a trilateral summit of Japan, China, and South Korea.

**XI JINPING'S GUARDIAN SPIRIT**

Why? What does he hope to accomplish?

**SHAKU**

Last time, in May last year, Japan, China, and South Korea discussed issues like the problem with North Korea and...

**XI JINPING'S G.S.**

There's nothing really to talk about.

**SHAKU**

I believe that is true.

**XI JINPING'S G.S.**

Yeah. There's nothing to discuss.

**SHAKU**
So, in regard to Japan, you're not really...

**XI JINPING'S G.S.**
Hmm?

**AYAORI**
Aren't you currently trying to rebuild the Chinese economy by improving China's economic ties with Japan?

**XI JINPING'S G.S.**
[*Sneers.*] Japan is nothing to us. What are you talking about? We are interacting with the entire world.

**AYAORI**
Hmm... If you continue with that approach, as there are more bankruptcies occurring domestically within China.

**XI JINPING'S G.S.**
Listen, once China starts to strangle with the U.S. through trade, the U.S. will then just demand Japan to make purchases to cover their losses. And before long, that will cause Japan to start disliking the U.S. The Japan-U.S. Alliance won't last for much longer.

**AYAORI**
Looking at the current situation objectively, it is clear that, for the last 30 years or so, China had been surviving by

making money in the U.S. But at the present time, it has become a lot harder to do business in the U.S. and you can no longer make money there. Isn't that right?

**XI JINPING'S G.S.**
No, that's not the case at all. We have so much money that we are thinking about buying up Alaska.

**AYAORI**
I doubt that you have enough money to buy Alaska.

**XI JINPING'S G.S.**
If we bought Alaska and built a missile base there, the U.S. would tremble in fear.

**AYAORI**
You are running short of money, and money is not circulating well in China, either.

**XI JINPING'S G.S.**
No, we have money. We have more than enough.

**AYAORI**
You also don't have enough money for your so-called "One Belt, One Road" Initiative.

**XI JINPING'S G.S.**
I said we have more than enough.

**AYAORI**

No. No, you don't. Not now. You've lost it all.

**SHAKU**

So, you didn't know that the renminbi (Chinese yuan) are flowing non-stop out of your country?

**XI JINPING'S G.S.**

No, no. The world revolves around China. So, next, instead of renminbi, I should issue a currency that has a portrait of Xi Jinping on it.

**AYAORI**

It would just be a piece of paper [*laughs*]. There's nothing that guarantees it.

**XI JINPING'S G.S.**

No, no, no. China has already entered the world of e-money, so that kind of thing won't be an issue. If China says it's good, then it's good. It's based on credibility. And the fact that the president is a god is what guarantees all of that credibility.

**AYAORI**

I see. That "guarantee" has almost no credibility [*laughs*], so it's difficult.

**XI JINPING'S G.S.**

You are an island nation, so your way of thinking is very narrow. But that's inevitable. You're such a tiny little country that you should just close yourself off and let the world forget about you.

***Next year's visit to Japan as a state guest is to preview whether or not to allow the Japanese imperial household to continue***

**AYAORI**

I have another question about Japan. I have heard that you are scheduled to visit Japan next year as a state guest. What will your purpose be at that time?

**XI JINPING'S G.S.**

Hmm. It will be to preview whether or not to allow the Japanese imperial household to continue.

**AYAORI**

You are coming to preview?

**XI JINPING'S G.S.**

Yes.

**SHAKU**

The imperial household?

## XI JINPING'S G.S.

Yes. I'm going there for a preview. I'm currently considering whether to let them continue or not.

## AYAORI

You will be a state guest, so naturally, you will meet with the new emperor and empress. Is that what you mean?

## XI JINPING'S G.S.

Yes. Right. I want to see what they are like.

## AYAORI

You're going to see what they are like?

## XI JINPING'S G.S.

Yes. I will be there to inspect whether they will be the last monarchy in Japan or not.

## AYAORI

Do you mean you intend to make them your subjects?

## XI JINPING'S G.S.

Yes. If I wanted to right now, I could subvert Japan.

## SHAKU

Prime Minister Abe has now been in office for an extremely long time.

**XI JINPING'S G.S.**
No. Actually, Prime Minister Abe isn't even supported by the majority of the citizens. His approval rating is only around 20%. Don't try to put me on the same level as such a weak prime minister.

**SHAKU**
Who do you think would be an appropriate prime minister after Mr. Abe?

**XI JINPING'S G.S.**
There isn't anyone.

**SHAKU**
No one?

**XI JINPING'S G.S.**
Not among these "villagers."

**SHAKU**
So, it doesn't matter who comes after him?

**XI JINPING'S G.S.**
I have no interest whatsoever in a "village chief election."

**SHAKU**

Soon, Japan will host the Olympics (2020 Tokyo Olympics). Is China hoping to use that chance to somehow plot against Japan?

**XI JINPING'S G.S.**

Yes. It will probably be your last Olympics because your country will disappear. We are soon going to take control of Hong Kong and Taiwan, and then Japan, Vietnam and the Philippines. We will conquer all of these areas and, when we take Guam and Hawaii, we will need to deal a blow to the U.S. We need to show them that they would not be able to win a war against us. By that time, we will need to have more than twice their economic power.

**AYAORI**

Hmm, that doesn't seem very likely from an objective point of view.

### *"Governor of Okinawa Tamaki is excellent," "Chinese domestic law is international law"*

**AYAORI**

This is about Japan again, but what do you think about Okinawa right now?

**XI JINPING'S G.S.**

I don't see any problems. Okinawa is anti-Japan, right? So, there's no problem.

**AYAORI**

Mr. Denny Tamaki is the new governor there. He says that he wants to make Okinawa the entrance into the "One Belt, One Road."

**XI JINPING'S G.S.**

Hmm, that's fine, I think. Yeah, he's excellent.

**SHAKU**

In connection with your current goal of "One Belt, One Road," there has been a series of cases in which a country has received funding from China, exactly as promised, but then is effectively transformed into a colony. This is the Chinese debt trap. In Japan, Haruhiko Kuroda, governor of the Bank of Japan, and others are working hard to prevent it, and there has been more and more instances where Japan provides funding instead of China. How do you view this situation?

**XI JINPING'S G.S.**

[*Sneers.*] You are so stupid. You're too slow. You are truly decades behind China. You end up following in China's footsteps, but just way later. You're stupid.

## SHAKU

What China is doing and what Japan is doing are not the same.

## XI JINPING'S G.S.

All you are doing is just interpreting. We loan money to places that don't have any, you know? And if they can't pay it back, it makes perfect sense for us to own them. There is no problem with that at all.

## SHAKU

That is exactly how the mafia operates.

## XI JINPING'S G.S.

It's international law. That's how international law operates.

## SHAKU

That is not how international law operates. That's how the mafia operates.

## XI JINPING'S G.S.

It's international law. If a country borrows money... We lend them money because they want it. So, we are meeting their needs. And if they can't pay it back, then it is perfectly natural for us to seize their property. Chinese domestic law is international law. There is no difference whatsoever.

# 5

# China's Diplomatic Policy On Major Powers

## *On the U.S.: China will triumph in the areas of space force and the 5G communication network*

AYAORI

You just said you'll make the U.S. see that they won't be able to win...

XI JINPING'S G.S.

You do get it, don't you? Well?

AYAORI

But President Trump is now trying to create a space force, strengthen cyber-related capabilities, and also develop missiles. Up until now, the U.S. stated that it wouldn't have any intermediate-range missiles, but now they scraped the treaty with Russia and tries to develop missiles, which will basically be deployed against China. This shows that the U.S. is trying to rebuild sectors where China has become strong and gain even stronger power to overtake China.

XI JINPING'S G.S.

The thing is, the U.S. has fallen behind.

**AYAORI**

Well, in some ways, yes.

**XI JINPING'S G.S.**

China is more advanced. The U.S. has finally realized that it is losing to China.

**AYAORI**

I think that is partly true.

**XI JINPING'S G.S.**

Its national goal is to somehow catch up with and over-take China. But we are ahead when it comes to space force, you know.

**AYAORI**

I can quite see that.

**XI JINPING'S G.S.**

We are capable of shooting down all satellites of the U.S. in one fell swoop. Once the satellites are down, their Aegis system is utterly destroyed. So, their missiles won't fly. It will all be over without a fight. The U.S. is really lagging behind. They didn't even notice the interference in their presidential election. All the phone calls of their important people are being tapped and they don't even know that either.

**AYAORI**

That is what 5G is aiming for, isn't it? The goal is for Huawei Technologies to dominate the world and gain control of all the data. Is that right?

**XI JINPING'S G.S.**

The U.S. is finished. To all intents and purposes, it has been left behind. We just wait for it to become physically obvious to the world. It's already finished.

**AYAORI**

But the U.S. is trying to eliminate Huawei Technologies globally.

**XI JINPING'S G.S.**

That's impossible. An economic bloc with 1.4 billion people cannot be ignored. By globalizing, companies must now yield to China. That's why the U.S. is trying to go back to unilateralism to protect their companies. Trump is trying to go back to the 19th century.

### *On Russia: The only way for Russia to survive is following China's lead*

**SHAKU**

Could you please tell us your thoughts on President Putin?

## XI JINPING'S G.S.

Well, he can be the logistical and military support for us in case of crisis. Russia sees the EU as a potential enemy, and vice versa; the EU also sees Russia as a potential enemy.

The U.S. have started to intervene the EU to make it collapse and are trying to split off the U.K. from it. I think they intend to create a "tiny community" with three countries—the U.S., Canada and the U.K., but of course they won't have a hope of beating us. We intend to swallow up the EU, the whole of Asia, and then the whole of Africa as well. The only way for Russia to survive will be to follow China's lead.

## SHAKU

President Putin is quite pro-Japanese. He once proposed to Prime Minister Abe, in the presence of President Xi Jinping, that they conclude a Russo-Japanese peace treaty.

## XI JINPING'S G.S.

They are forever negotiating, right? That would be an endless negotiations.

## SHAKU

How do you see that situation?

## XI JINPING'S G.S.

I'm not interested in the negotiations of small fry. It's just ridiculous. While you want the four northern islands, do you want to sign a peace treaty? That's absolutely inconsistent.

The thing is, your national delegates have no authority. It's a mistake to believe in such an idea as "the sovereignty of the people." You should just trample over that. How can you get anything done like that? Only one person should have sovereignty. And that's fine. Is Japan's Emperor mere window dressing? As I doubt that Abe runs the country successfully with the approval rating of only about 20%, next year I'm going to test how strong the Emperor actually is and I will crush its whole system, too, if I see I can.

### On the Middle East: The oil supply is the main point

## SHAKU

How about the relationship with Iran?

## XI JINPING'S G.S.

There are many countries, and we don't really have any specific nations in mind as long as they produce oil. It doesn't matter from who we get oil, as long as they supply it to us. And if they can't, we'll just attack them. We'll attack and take over the whole country. That's all.

**SHAKU**

How about Israel? You have a military connection via arms sales.

**XI JINPING'S G.S.**

It's too small to matter. I have no interest in them. The U.S. seems to be supporting Israel because Trump's son-in-law is Jewish. Mr. Trump has a tendency to consider things in terms of personal friendships, which proves his unintelligence. Basically, that is small-town thinking. Well, I don't think he's smart. He won't make the cut in the global community with that level of intelligence.

## On Canada, Italy, Greece and France

**FUJII**

You mentioned Canada earlier. I guess you are very interested in Canada, given that it is a great immigration nation with many Chinese immigrants.

**XI JINPING'S G.S.**

I'm now thinking about how to invade Canada, because we need to dissociate it.

**AYAORI**

Does it mean you're going to use Canada?

**XI JINPING'S G.S.**

It doesn't count as a developed country. At the G7, countries like Canada and Italy are just there on sufferance.

**AYAORI**

Are you saying that you will use Canada for invasion?

**XI JINPING'S G.S.**

I'm gradually setting to work on Canada, of course.

**AYAORI**

Is that a maneuver against the U.S.?

**XI JINPING'S G.S.**

Obviously, it's a good idea to have America's neighbors on our side. We can get Italy and Greece as well, and France is ripe for the picking, so I intend to get France too.

## On India: From China's perspective, India is lagging 500 years behind

**SHAKU**

India is becoming increasingly vigilant because it sees the One Belt, One Road Initiative as a scheme to encircle it. In terms of population, some people predict that India will outstrip China and...

## XI JINPING'S G.S.

Even if it outstrips us, [*laughs*] an undeveloped country like that hasn't got a hope.

## SHAKU

So, you think there is no likelihood of it becoming a genuine opposing force?

## XI JINPING'S G.S.

About half its population can't even go to elementary school, can they? Anyway, it's a country where they put the cow dung on the walls of their homes, dry it in the sun and then use it as fuel. That's just, well... From a Chinese perspective, the country is lagging around 500 years behind, I suppose.

## On Taiwan: Annexing Taiwan in the lifetime of the current generation

## AYAORI

There is one thing that worries me about your earlier remarks on Taiwan. You said something on the lines of having "switched" a candidate, and I guess you were talking about Mr. Han Kuo-yu. Is it correct to understand that you switched the Kuomintang candidate and are supporting Mr. Han Kuo-yu?

## XI JINPING'S G.S.

You Japan is so lagging behind that you just can't get it. We carry out cyber-attacks and change public opinions in various places.

## AYAORI

Ah, I see. It is said that various fake news circulate extensively due to the cyber-attack. So, you are saying that you used it to change the public opinions.

## XI JINPING'S G.S.

Exactly. Japan is also under attack, but there's little influence in Japan because it's still an undeveloped country. It will be easier to manipulate if it becomes a little more advanced. You will see how we swallow up Taiwan, because it will happen in your lifetime. And you will be on the menu after Taiwan.

## AYAORI

When Master Okawa gave a lecture in Taiwan this March,* you (Xi Jinping's G.S.) demanded that he cancel the lecture and tried to obstruct him.

---

* On March 3, 2019, Okawa gave a lecture, "Ai wa Nikushimi wo Koete" (lit. "Love Beyond Hatred") at Grand Hyatt Taipei, Taiwan. See Chapter 3 in Ryuho Okawa, *Love for the Future* (New York: IRH Press, 2019).

## XI JINPING'S G.S.

No, that kind of work is handled by the underlings.

## AYAORI

[*Smiles wryly.*] Really? I think it was you.

## FUJII

On the day of the lecture, Mr. Xi Jinping (his guardian spirit) came to tell us to cancel the lecture.

## AYAORI

Mr. Xi Jinping an "underling"—is that what you mean?

## XI JINPING'S G.S.

No, no, no. It really was the work of an underling.

## AYAORI

Actually, no. You were very upset about it.

## XI JINPING'S G.S.

A "small" lecture like that can't have any effect at all on mighty China. We have 1.4 billion people! Yours was a lecture in a hotel with just an audience of less than a thousand.

**AYAORI**

So, you were upset about such a "small" lecture?

**XI JINPING'S G.S.**

What? A lecture in Japanese has no impact at all. Zero influence, or thereabouts.

**AYAORI**

But you were upset about what was going to be said at the lecture, right?

**XI JINPING'S G.S.**

It was totally in vain. It had absolutely no impact.

**AYAORI**

You were upset because that lecture would work to protect Taiwan, protect Hong Kong, and transform China, is that right?

**XI JINPING'S G.S.**

You had your tiny publishing company. You had a couple of employees in Beijing, but they have fled and the company was dissolved. They ran away, didn't they? Weaklings.

**AYAORI**

Actually, no. You were really upset about it.

**XI JINPING'S G.S.**
Huh. Weaklings.

**FUJII**
You came to Master and spent around 13 minutes telling him to cancel the lecture.

**XI JINPING'S G.S.**
I'm keeping an eye on the whole world, so that kind of thing might happen sometimes, but I'm too busy to remember stuff like that.

**AYAORI**
Surely it was an important task, because you took the trouble to come to negotiate when you are so busy.

**XI JINPING'S G.S.**
Absolutely not. It wasn't important at all. We sorted you out in the House of Councilors election, right? You lost votes and are now driven to the point of extinction, right? The anti-NHK party got more votes, didn't it? You are already finished.

# 6

## "Infection by the West is a Sickness"

### *Democratization will lead to a decline in the ability to rule*

**AYAORI**

Master Okawa once said that if Hong Kong tried hard, it might be able to bring China to democratize, that they could throw China down as if using a suplex move in a wrestling match.* That's what you want to prevent, is that right?

**XI JINPING'S G.S.**

That's impossible. Simply impossible. We just have to kill a few leaders and it will all be over.

**AYAORI**

No, Mr. Joshua Wong also says that more leaders will emerge, one after another; that they will come forth more.

---

* On May 22, 2011, Okawa gave an English lecture, "The Fact and the Truth" in Hong Kong and called for the people in Hong Kong to be the standard-bearer of China's reform. Similar messages have been continually given even after that. See Chapter 2 in the aforementioned *Love for the Future*.

## XI JINPING'S G.S.
Killing doesn't necessarily mean murder. It's just that some "accident" will happen.

## AYAORI
Well, I suppose that's how you usually do. But a series of people have actually emerged from out of those millions, and they are determined to democratize China.

## XI JINPING'S G.S.
You talk about democratization as if it's a good thing, but from our point of view, as far as we know, it is nothing but a decline in the ability to rule.

## SHAKU
Isn't it China that is experiencing a decline in its ability to rule?

## XI JINPING'S G.S.
I heard that the movie, *Kingdom*\*, is now popular in your country. You ought to have understood how important it is to unify a country.

---

\* A Japanese film released in 2019. It is a story of a war-orphaned boy who aims to become a king in the Spring and Autumn and Warring States periods in China.

AYAORI

One issue that has been discussed in the Hong Kong protests is of course the democratization of Hong Kong, but there is also a discussion of exporting democratization to China.

XI JINPING'S G.S.

No thanks, we don't need it. If they did it, we would simply nuke them. The movement would dissolve with the death of seven million people.

AYAORI

But I think it would also lead to the end of China, if you truly did so.

SHAKU

I heard in Hong Kong that movements seeking democracy are spreading inside mainland China as well.

XI JINPING'S G.S.

Well, if they make too much noise, we'll just drop a nuclear bomb on all areas, including Hong Kong, Xinjiang Uyghur, Tibet and Inner Mongolia, as an experiment.

## FUJII

I'm afraid it is probably your position that is actually becoming precarious.

## XI JINPING'S G.S.

No. You should realize that "being infected by the West" is a state of sickness. It's a disease. All countries that have westernized have gone into decline.

### No one can remonstrate with Mr. Xi Jinping and accurate information fails to reach him

## AYAORI

I suppose you are now surrounded only by the most trusted aides, and scarcely any accurate information reaches you. You just receive information that's pleasant to hear, don't you?

## XI JINPING'S G.S.

But who are you to say that? Only a writer of a magazine that doesn't sell, aren't you?

## AYAORI

I feel really sorry for you.

**XI JINPING'S G.S.**

At least I have the information that your magazine doesn't sell.

**AYAORI**

Well, we'll do our best on that.

**XI JINPING'S G.S.**

From what I've heard, its circulation keeps dropping, doesn't it? Because you distribute information for free.

**AYAORI**

It seems that the weakness of being a dictator is becoming evident, and you are no longer able to see your own situation and you don't seem to understand what's going on.

**XI JINPING'S G.S.**

Well, your Happiness Realization Party or Happy Science, or whatever, seems to have sent a message to Hong Kong, saying "Japan will support you," but you're simply showing how powerless you are. You'll just end up destroying yourself.

**AYAORI**

Actually, no. People who learned about Master's message in Taiwan are fighting in Hong Kong. Many people have understood Master Okawa's lecture and carry out the movement.

## XI JINPING'S G.S.
Hah. Don't act big overseas when you can't win in Japan.

## SHAKU
But it has become a battle of philosophies.

## XI JINPING'S G.S.
Just don't come to Canada! You're not wanted there.

## AYAORI
Aha, are you worried about Canada as well?

## XI JINPING'S G.S.
There's no point in going to Canada because there's nothing there except beavers and reindeer!

## AYAORI
So, you want to add Canada to your territories?

## XI JINPING'S G.S.
There are only beavers, reindeers and timber. Nothing else.

## SHAKU

What scares you the most is Master Okawa's lectures. I clearly see that now.

## XI JINPING'S G.S.

I'm not. I'm not scared at all. Not even a little bit. If he goes to a Chinese restaurant with you and tries to speak in Chinese, then that will be scary. It will indeed be scary if he starts to give a lecture in vulgar conversational Chinese. That would be so scary.

# 7

# Ambition to be Greater than Mao Zedong and the First Emperor of Qin Dynasty

## *"I'll take advantage of Mao Zedong as long as I can"*

**AYAORI**

I'd like to ask you about spiritual matters. Last November, we recorded a spiritual message from Mao Zedong, and it revealed that Mao Zedong is the greatest Devil on Earth. Do you sometimes converse with Mao Zedong, receive instructions from him, or hear his words?

**XI JINPING'S G.S.**

Actually, Mao Zedong is really just a paper tiger. I have to sing his praises at the moment because he found the Communist Party, but soon everyone will recognize that I'm superior to him. At that time, I'll have no use for him. He may well be discarded before long.

**SHAKU**

So, you don't admire him as someone of the same lineage or, how do I say, as a forerunner...

**XI JINPING'S G.S.**
Well, I take advantage of him while he's still useful, but I won't need him any longer once I've established my authority.

**SHAKU**
So, who do you respect?

**XI JINPING'S G.S.**
No one, of course.

**SHAKU**
No one?

**XI JINPING'S G.S.**
Mm. Because I am the best. It's obvious.

### Like Japan's Abe, I will get rid of people regarded as my successor

**FUJII**
The person predicted to be your successor...

**XI JINPING'S G.S.**
There's no such person. No successor.

**FUJII**
There's not?

**XI JINPING'S G.S.**
I, well... didn't I tell you?

**AYAORI**
In your last spiritual message, you said you were considering a person who could be your successor.

**XI JINPING'S G.S.**
I don't consider that at all. Well, when it comes to successors, I'm actually the same as Mr. Abe. We're the same in that anyone who is expected to be a successor will "disappear." That's one of the characteristics of those in power. Mr. Abe also gets rid of anyone whose name is mentioned as a possible successor. Yes, we're the same about that.

**FUJII**
You don't seem to worry about any possibility of political change...

**XI JINPING'S G.S.**
I'm not worried about it in the slightest. Anyone who would attempt it would be dead before anything should happen. I have an excellent surveillance network in place, so I have no worries about that.

**FUJII**

But I've heard that there have already been a number of attempts to assassinate Mr. Xi Jinping.

**XI JINPING'S G.S.**

Well, there have been a few, but I've killed a far greater number of people.

**"It's ridiculous that Christianity has given its two billion believers sovereign authority and human rights!"**

**AYAORI**

You don't seem to have an objective view of your own situation. And given that you obviously terminate any potential enemy, we can clearly see that you loathe religion the most.

**XI JINPING'S G.S.**

Mmm.

**AYAORI**

You wipe out every religion in mainland China, be it Christianity, Buddhism or Taoism, not to mention Uyghurs. You destroy churches and temples, and send believers to jail. So, you loathe religion the most, is that right?

**XI JINPING'S G.S.**
I guess I feel like Nobunaga. That's normal.

**AYAORI**
So, you fear religious organizations and people's faith?

**XI JINPING'S G.S.**
Anyone who defies the government must be kicked out.
After all, it's vital to unify the nation.

**AYAORI**
The Hong Kong Chief Executive Carrie Lam is also a
Catholic. Earlier we talked about the Catholic believers
singing hymns as they march...

**XI JINPING'S G.S.**
Well, someone as powerful as me can have Christ killed,
however many times he appears. That's nothing [*laughs*].
He can never defeat me in this world.

**AYAORI**
But because of her faith in Catholicism, Ms. Carrie Lam
has a wish to resign as chief executive, and in some ways
she is already resisting the government in Beijing.

## XI JINPING'S G.S.

She should be crucified then. She could be burnt to death on a cross at a protest rally. Maybe she could become a bit of a saint that way.

## AYAORI

It is said that she went to see a bishop to make confession after the June 9 protest march of more than a million people.

## XI JINPING'S G.S.

How pathetic. You'd better know that, in this world, I'm superior to Christ. And I'm aiming for that in the other world as well. I believe it will happen.

## AYAORI

But I'm sure your biggest enemy would be the forces of religious people.

## XI JINPING'S G.S.

Christianity claims to have two to 2.2 billion believers, which slightly outnumbers China.

## SHAKU

It isn't a matter of numbers actually. You don't seem to understand this point at all.

**XI JINPING'S G.S.**
What?

**SHAKU**
From the perspective of someone who knows religions, including Christianity, you are not a great man at all. Are you not aware of that?

**XI JINPING'S G.S.**
You're part of the "rebel army," just by saying that.

**SHAKU**
No. That is the truth from eyes of anyone who believes in God, whether they are a Muslim or a Christian.

**XI JINPING'S G.S.**
That's ridiculous. It's nonsense to hand over sovereign authority to two billion people. Two billion people with sovereign authority? That would just be an unruly mob, wouldn't it?

**SHAKU**
Hong Kong is now precisely confronting the issue of sovereignty, like security issue.

**XI JINPING'S G.S.**
The West is full of liars. They say things like, "Sovereignty lies with the people," "It belongs to everyone," or "There are fundamental human rights," but those are all lies. After all, sovereignty is in the hands of those in power. That is how it is everywhere.

**SHAKU**
I see. Then, surely, that old way of thinking that those in power have sovereignty...

**XI JINPING'S G.S.**
It's not old. It's new. Even if someone were to become a Darth Vader in the future, he will have the power.

**SHAKU**
That old way of thinking is going to be washed away with the flow of time. This kind of huge scale-drama has already been unfolding on a global level. Maybe you should really be aware of that, I suppose.

**XI JINPING'S G.S.**
The U.S. can never beat China in space force. All the American systems are set to be destroyed. That's why they have started to intervene Huawei Technologies. Before

long... Well, we need to be patient a little bit longer. We still have to be patient just a little longer, until around 2025 or 2030, but once I can see the complete victory we'll launch into action around the world.

## AYAORI

I'm afraid to say that you don't seem to perceive the situation correctly.

## XI JINPING'S G.S.

Do I? Just like your magazine (the monthly magazine *The Liberty*).

## AYAORI

The U.S. have shown favor to China to a certain extent since the last world war. They continued to do so during the cold war with the Soviet Union. Basically, there was a certain degree of cooperative relationship between the U.S. and China, but since Mr. Trump became president, this trend has changed. The U.S. have completely cut the aid and are ready to confront China.

## XI JINPING'S G.S.

You'd better not to trust the U.S. They said they would strike out at Japan as their enemy and would assist China.

**AYAORI**
Well, yes, that's partly true.

**XI JINPING'S G.S.**
After that, they have joined forces with Japan and started to attack China, haven't they? They once joined forces with Iraq to fight the Iranian Revolution, but then they destroyed Iraq, and now they're trying to crush Iran, too. It's a country that can't be relied on.

**AYAORI**
It's true that there is that side to the U.S. We are aware of that.

**XI JINPING'S G.S.**
You shouldn't believe a word they say.

**SHAKU**
It is our Lord who considers the trend of the times, the direction in which the world—including the U.S. and China—should head into. I have strongly felt from today's session that the grand current of the times has been created on Earth just right now.

**XI JINPING'S G.S.**
Mm. Well, in any case, I want my name to go down in history as someone greater than the First Emperor of Qin

Dynasty, so I'm determined to accomplish considerable work accordingly.

## SHAKU
While you say you want to outdo the First Emperor of Qin Dynasty, to be perfectly honest, he is far from being categorized as a great man of virtue.

## XI JINPING'S G.S.
Mm. Hmm. Well, but his name has lasted for two thousand years.

## SHAKU
So, you just want your name to last a long time?

## XI JINPING'S G.S.
Hmm. What do you mean?

## SHAKU
For your name to be remembered, even as someone evil.

## XI JINPING'S G.S.
Exactly. Everyone knows the First Emperor of Qin Dynasty. I'm not sure if Mao Zedong's name would still be known two thousand years from now.

## The role of Xi Jinping's daughter in creating a surveillance nation

**FUJII**

According to Happy Science spiritual research, the soul of Kublai Khan has most probably been born somewhere. Do you have any idea who that might be? This person could be even greater than Genghis Khan.[*]

**XI JINPING'S G.S.**

Mm, that might be my daughter.

**FUJII**

Ah.

**SHAKU**

Are you saying that Kublai Khan might have been born as a female?

**XI JINPING'S G.S.**

I say this because my daughter is currently working on a cyber-revolution.

---

[*] A previous spiritual research by Happy Science hinted that one of the past lives of Mr. Xi Jinping is Genghis Khan, the first Khagan of the Mongol Empire.

**SHAKU**
Ah. So, since she came back from her study in the U.S., you consider her to be a de facto successor...

**XI JINPING'S G.S.**
That's not what I mean. While I'm trying to create a nation with total surveillance, I don't know anything about computers, so it's my daughter who is taking control of everything.

**FUJII**
Ah.

**XI JINPING'S G.S.**
That means she's much cleverer than Trump's daughter, you know.

**SHAKU**
So, we will be seeing more of her from now on, won't we?

**FUJII**
Does it mean you are thinking on the lines of imperial succession?

**XI JINPING'S G.S.**
The possibility is not zero... Actually, I can't go into details

about the future. My daughter does have some authority, but I'm not sure about the rest at the moment.

## SHAKU

Are you saying that your daughter is the only one you can trust?

## XI JINPING'S G.S.

[*Laughs.*] The thing is, she's made China the most advanced country in the field that I'm the least good at. She's created an amazing flawless system where 1.4 billion people are placed under total surveillance.

## SHAKU

That is incredible.

## XI JINPING'S G.S.

Yes. Look at Japan. When a criminal is on the run, the case is followed on TV for a week, or maybe two, isn't it? You don't know who has done wrong on the streets, you don't know where a suspect who stabbed a police officer fled to. But in China, that can be computed just in 10 minutes. There's nowhere to run.

## SHAKU

Your daughter has created such a surveillance society; you would really...

**XI JINPING'S G.S.**
You may think you can enter Hong Kong easily because your passport is under another name, but be careful. You may be in danger next.

**SHAKU**
Yes, I'm aware of that.

**XI JINPING'S G.S.**
You have been marked.

**SHAKU**
Thank you for that interesting information.

**XI JINPING'S G.S.**
Mm. Well, perhaps you're lucky. Since your name is unknown in Japan, you could get burnt with gasoline in Hong Kong, or maybe just half-burnt would be enough to make you very famous.

**SHAKU**
No, thank you.

# 8
# Message to Ms. Agnes Chow

## *"Ask Agnes's guardian spirit how she wants to die"*

**AYAORI**
I am sorry, but today's main guest is Ms. Agnes Chow.
[*Audience laughs.*]

**XI JINPING'S G.S.**
What?

**AYAORI**
She is scheduled after this.

**XI JINPING'S G.S.**
What do you think you can do with such an "untitled" person?

**AYAORI**
Well, if you have any messages for Ms. Agnes Chow...

**XI JINPING'S G.S.**
Well, as an act of mercy for her, I will teach her "how to die." I'll allow her to choose how she wants to die, so ask

her that. I know she will die, but as my "last act of mercy" I will allow her to choose how she will die.

**AYAORI**

I think she has already put her life at stake from the outset.

**XI JINPING'S G.S.**

I doubt it, because she wanted to be released on bail.

**AYAORI**

I don't think that's her real intention.

**XI JINPING'S G.S.**

She was released on bail of 130,000 yen. That means she wanted to save her life.

It's already been decided that she will be killed. I've already decided, so I'll just allow her to choose how she will die—how she wants to die.

**AYAORI**

I will tell her that.

**XI JINPING'S G.S.**

Yes, ask her. I'm sure she will beg for her life.

**AYAORI**

Thank you very much for telling us in detail today about your thoughts on Hong Kong and other ambitions you have.

**XI JINPING'S G.S.**

I question your idea to position (the guardian spirit of) Agnes Chow on the same spot as myself. I mean, our statuses are worlds apart.

**AYAORI**

We would like to judge that in an objective manner.

**XI JINPING'S G.S.**

Even if this was, for example, "Chinese President Xi Jinping vs Chairperson of Happy Science," it would still be embarrassing to make it into a book to publish. Right?

**AYAORI**

I don't think so.

**XI JINPING'S G.S.**

You should feel embarrassed. That's natural.

**SHAKU**

I'm a little disappointed to hear your "boring story."

**XI JINPING'S G.S.**

What? It's simply that you are stupid. That's it! As simple as that.

**SHAKU**

[*Laughs.*] Umm...

**XI JINPING'S G.S.**

I'm a graduate of China's number one university (Tsinghua University).

**SHAKU**

You say China's number one university... Is that...? [*Laughs.*]

**XI JINPING'S G.S.**

I graduated when I was around 26 with excellent grades. I am an elite.

**SHAKU**

I see.

**AYAORI**

Well, thank you very much.

**XI JINPING'S G.S.**

Yes.

**AYAORI**

I think you will be busy in September and October.

**XI JINPING'S G.S.**

Yes, really busy.

**AYAORI**

I hope you will take a good look at your own situation.

**XI JINPING'S G.S.**

Will you stop annoying me like flies buzzing around me?

**AYAORI**

I'm afraid we can't.

**XI JINPING'S G.S.**

Even if you translate this (spiritual message), I mean... You just can sell a few copies in Taiwan and Hong Kong, right? It will not be circulated at all, even in Chinese.

**AYAORI**

Actually no, we will spread it around the world.

## XI JINPING'S G.S.

It will not circulate in mainland China. If it did, I would arrest everyone involved. Anyway, your president (of IRH Press) is no good. You really should replace him with a Chinese guy. Maybe then, it may spread to China.

## AYAORI

Mr. Xi Jinping's real intention will run through the world, so we are sure to spread this.

## "I am president for life. I will still be a president even after Trump is gone"

## XI JINPING'S G.S.

Hmph. I can see the U.S. have gained confidence than before but I can see the end of the U.S. already. It already ended the moment I became president for life. Even after Mr. Trump, I still am the Chinese president. Even after the Trump's term, I will still be here. The next American president will most likely be anti-Trump, so at that time, the U.S. will bow before China. This is a prophecy, so make sure you write this down.

## AYAORI

I think, at this time, you are just overconfident.

**SHAKU**

I clearly see that you fail to understand that capable people can spring from anywhere in a world of freedom, democracy, and faith.

**XI JINPING'S G.S.**

Pretty soon, we will be saying good-bye to Mr. Trump, and the Happiness Realization Party will only gain about 10,000 votes at the next election and "disappear."

**SHAKU**

Say all you want.

**AYAORI**

OK. Thank you very much. Our main guest is waiting in the wings. [*Audience laughs.*]

**XI JINPING'S G.S.**

Ahh. I see.

**AYAORI**

Yes. Thank you very much.

**XI JINPING'S G.S.**

OK then. OK.

# 9

## After the Spiritual Message: He Feels All Will End if He Shows Any Weakness

**RYUHO OKAWA**
[*Claps four times.*]

**AYAORI**
Thank you very much.

**RYUHO OKAWA**
Thank you. His way of talking was a bit more like a villain than he was previously. I guess he feels irritated. Like the president of South Korea, he probably is rather unpleasant.

**AYAORI**
I think so, too. They had a similar vibe.

**RYUHO OKAWA**
I guess he cannot really reveal his true thoughts. He probably feels that all will end for him if he shows any weakness.

# Chapter Two

# Spiritual Messages from the Guardian Spirit of Agnes Chow Ting

Recorded September 3, 2019
General Headquarters, Happy Science
Japan

# Agnes Chow Ting (1996 -present)

A Hong Kong social activist. Enrolled at Hong Kong Baptist University. She played a central role during the Umbrella Revolution in 2014, and has been referred to as "the Goddess of Democracy." In 2016, she was one of the founding members of the political party, Demosisto, among other student leaders. In 2018, her bid to run for the Legislative Council by-election was banned by the Hong Kong government. In June of 2019, she participated in a massive protest march against the extradition law amendments. She continues to call for international support for the pro-democracy movement in Hong Kong.

## Interviewers from Happy Science[*]:

### Jiro Ayaori

Managing Director
Director General of Magazine Editing Division
Chief Editor of *The Liberty*
Lecturer at Happy Science University

### Ryoko Shaku

Party Leader
Happiness Realization Party

### Motohisa Fujii

Associate Director
Special Assistant to Religious Affairs Headquarters
Director General of International Politics Division

*No statements made by the guardian spirit of Ms. Agnes Chow Ting in this book reflect statements actually made by Ms. Chow herself.*

*The opinions of the spirit do not necessarily reflect those of Happy Science Group. For the mechanism behind spiritual messages, see end section.*

---

[*] Interviewers are listed in the order that they appear in the transcript. Their professional titles represent their positions at the time of the interview.

# 1

## "I Might Throw Up from The Smell of an Old Man"

### *"We need an exorcism for the guardian spirit of Xi Jinping"*

**RYUHO OKAWA**

Shall we move on to Ms. Agnes Chow then? We would like to summon the guardian spirit of Ms. Agnes Chow Ting, one of the leaders of Hong Kong who is referred to as "the Goddess of Democracy." Ms. Agnes Chow, please come down to the Happy Science General Headquarters and share your opinions on Xi Jinping's thoughts and the ideal state of self-governance in Hong Kong. We would greatly appreciate it.

Ms. Agnes Chow, Ms. Agnes Chow. You may be busy, but will you kindly come to Happy Science and tell us your true thoughts?

*[About 10 seconds of silence.]*

**AGNES CHOW'S GUARDIAN SPIRIT**

There seemed to have been someone I don't like...

**AYAORI**

We apologize for that.

**AGNES CHOW'S G.S.**

Ahh. I don't like to be lumped with him.

**AYAORI**

We'd like to switch our focus as we proceed with this interview.

**AGNES CHOW'S G.S.**

Once again, I need... I'm not sure how to say it... Japanese is difficult. Ablution? Yes, I need an exorcism and a purification. Otherwise it feels uncomfortable.

**AYAORI**

Ah, I see. Right.

**AGNES CHOW'S G.S.**

You see, there is something unpleasant in the air. Please exorcise it. We really need an exorcism. An exorcism, an exorcism.

**AYAORI**

I think Ms. Agnes Chow Ting has a pure energy, indeed.

## AGNES CHOW'S G.S.

Ew, ew, ew, ew. Xi Jinping stinks, stinks. Stinky, stinky. Stinky, stinky. Smells of an old man. Hm, ugh, disgusting. Sigh, I don't like him. Ewww. [*Audience laughs*]. I feel like throwing up. I feel like throwing up.

## AYAORI

I understand how you might feel that way.

## *"It's better to cleanse such old ways of thinking"*

## SHAKU

I saw the protest march in Hong Kong firsthand and sensed that the people of the younger generation loathe Xi Jinping, just like you do now. I had a strong impression that they are greatly different from the younger generation in Japan.

## AGNES CHOW'S G.S.

It's too old, too old. Those ways of thinking are too old. It's better to stop thinking in that way. Yes, the Communist Party needs a cleansing. He is done for; someone sticking to such old ways of thinking is finished. He can't keep up with the new generation. He probably doesn't understand what we are doing. I bet he has never seen Japanese anime. He probably doesn't know anything about it.

It almost seems like he wants to become the next Cao Cao, in this age. I think he wants to follow in the footsteps of Cao Cao of the Three Kingdoms period. Don't you think?

## AYAORI
In that sense, I feel that Mr. Xi Jinping's decisions somehow have the opposite effect. He seems to be heading in the opposite direction of the current times.

## AGNES CHOW'S G.S.
Hmm, I don't know about heading in the opposite direction, but I'm sure his plans will fall apart at some point.

## AYAORI
Hmm.

## AGNES CHOW'S G.S.
Even so, he still has much power, and I believe he is doing everything he desires. He does things people hate, without hesitation. For instance, he interfered with the Taiwanese presidential election. I think he only sees Hong Kong as a "small fly" that buzzes around his head and disrupts his work. But that is our mission. We are pretty small in number; we are about one-two hundredth of their

population. But we are doing this, believing we are the "conscience" of China.

**SHAKU**
I see.

## Sinocentrism is stuck in ancient times and simply telling us to "pay tribute to the emperor"

**SHAKU**
Just a moment ago, you dismissed China as "old," but there are young people like you, who are of a new generation, expressing their innate leadership and taking action.

We see a lot of young people acting in solidarity. What do you perceive the mission of the young generation to be?

**AGNES CHOW'S G.S.**
Don't you think it's quite out-of-date to be ignorant of what other countries are thinking, especially at a time when information can be rampantly shared across the globe? They essentially can't perceive how their decisions and actions are viewed from a global perspective, right? Don't you think it's really behind the times?

This means Chinese Sinocentrism hasn't changed since the ancient times. Diplomacy in their eyes is for the world to follow the tributary system and continue to serve the "emperor" of China. That's pretty much all they are conveying. I suppose they want to restore such Sinocentrism once again. That's all.

## SHAKU
I totally agree.

## AGNES CHOW'S G.S.
They believe that the countries around the world paid tribute to China when it was at its height. They want to regain that status. Isn't this what they are implying?

# 2

# Representing the Movement with Her Face Uncovered Because She Has Already Come to Terms with Her Own Death

## *"We need someone who is willing to show their face"*

**SHAKU**

Ms. Agnes Chow and Mr. Joshua Wong were arrested the other day. Despite these attempts to intimidate them, it seems like they have no – shall we say – fear, whatsoever. And seeing their strength, I believe people around the world are being inspired by them. Where does this strength...?

**AGNES CHOW'S G.S.**

Well, I believe China's intention is for us to fear them, so we have to fight against it. Other people wear black masks and hide their faces, but I show my face. It's because we need someone who is willing to show their face. Of course, I am well aware of the danger of being arrested or killed, but I have already come to terms with it. That's the point of being a representative. Yes.

### *"Perhaps, he will be the one to die first?"*

**AYAORI**

The "vile" guardian spirit of Xi Jinping earlier said, "choose how (you) will die."

**AGNES CHOW'S G.S.**

Shouldn't he be the one to die first?

**AYAORI**

Ah, I see.

**AGNES CHOW'S G.S.**

Yes. He's pretty old already. He should be the one to think about it. Would he like to die from cancer? Or a myocardial infarction? What else? A stroke, maybe? What does he want to die from?

**AYAORI**

Well, I have heard rumors that there are plenty of people who want to assassinate him.

**AGNES CHOW'S G.S.**

In case he gets poisoned, he should always have someone taste his food ahead of time.

# 3

# Japan Prioritizes Economic Gain and is Not Trustworthy

## *"Japanese people don't have opinions. It's sad."*

### SHAKU

In regards to international support of Hong Kong, we see countries like the United States trying to pass a bill to protect Hong Kong's freedom. We understand that Ms. Agnes Chow has been a driving force in gaining more international support for Hong Kong and has visited Japan for the same reasons as well. What are your thoughts on this?

### AGNES CHOW'S G.S.

We've had Japanese news reporters from various TV stations and newspaper companies visit us for interviews, but even if they come for interviews... hmm... How do I say this? Even though Japan is nearby, the Japanese people do not have any specific opinions toward our movement. That's the sad part.

It's frustrating because we don't know if the opinions of the reporters will be directly reflected in their news stories. I think it would be great if the reporters' reactions could be broadcast directly, but I don't know how their reports actually turn out. This is where both Japanese TV stations and newspaper companies are untrustworthy, and is therefore very disappointing. In a way, Japan has some "China-like" qualities.

**SHAKU**

Japanese news media probably don't have the perspective that China is behind the times. Not only that, many people of certain generations still believe that China is their spiritual mother country.

## *The aim of meeting with Mr. Yamamoto and Mr. Edano, who share the same thoughts as China*

**SHAKU**

As seen in various pictures, when Ms. Agnes Chow came to Japan, she directly met with some Japanese politicians like Mr. Taro Yamamoto and Mr. Yukio Edano. In Japan, these politicians are known to share similar thoughts as China; they have contributed to the forces inviting China to replace the American bases in Okinawa. Did you meet these people without knowing those views?

**AGNES CHOW'S G.S.**

Well, Mr. Abe and his associates have their guards up; they don't want to get involved.

**SHAKU**

Ah, I see.

**AGNES CHOW'S G.S.**

They believe getting involved will only be disadvantageous to them. They wouldn't let their guard down for fear of causing losses to Japanese trade and economy, so I cannot get access to them. The only few Diet members who might be open to the idea of meeting us, were the ones I've already met. Perhaps they are leaning more toward China, but even so, by meeting them, China would become suspicious that Japan is on Hong Kong's side. So, it wasn't all bad.

**SHAKU**

I suppose it is a huge problem that Japan's Liberal Democratic Party won't lend an ear to you.

## The Liberal Democratic Party prioritizes economic gains over political decisions

**AGNES CHOW'S G.S.**

The priority of Japan's Liberal Democratic Party lies in economic gain. They put economic decisions before political ones. There is no one to take responsibility, nor does anyone want to. If we were to meet the Japanese Foreign Minister, it will immediately worsen relations with China, right? The same would be true with the Minister of Defense.

Well, earlier you were talking about immigrants, but the Japanese government is in a state where they can't even decide whether or not to take in immigrants from Hong Kong because they are too afraid to face accusations from China. That's most likely how the Japanese government is.

So, well... I've had an affinity toward Japan, but in regards to decision making and making judgements, I think Japan is a "disappointing" country and is a little difficult to negotiate with. I'm not quite sure who I should approach to set Japan into action.

# 4

# Dissemination of Information is About to be Quelled

## *"China is starting to block our interaction with international news media"*

### AYAORI
I see Ms. Agnes Chow continuously sending a lot of information in Japanese through social media like Twitter. Why do you care so much about communicating in Japanese? Is it correct to assume that you think Japan plays a big role in solving the issue with China?

### AGNES CHOW'S G.S.
I know there are many different ideas. There are close to 200 countries worldwide, but the most effective way to contain China would certainly be for the United States and Japan to encircle it. If these two countries strongly expressed their views, China couldn't totally ignore them.

### FUJII
According to the news, Ms. Agnes Chow's release on bail came with a condition of limited mobility. As a result, despite Ms. Agnes Chow's plans to visit Japan at the end

of the year, she can no longer come to Japan from now on. Is there anything you sense regarding the intentions of the Communist Party?

## AGNES CHOW'S G.S.

I think such restrictions will be imposed more and more. I believe they have already started the "containment" process. They will probably try to contain everything into one division of Hong Kong and prevent opinion and information from escaping that region.

It's also likely for foreign media coverage to be restricted as well. In regards to CNN though, since they are Mr. Trump's enemy, China would probably want to control them tactfully as anti-US media.

Domestic media is almost completely censored, and the remaining challenge for them is figure out how to "shut out" foreign media. One way to do this is to block us from having any interactions with foreign media. Once abroad, we can speak freely. But inside Hong Kong, they can increasingly keep a close watch on us and block our contact with foreign media; in this way they can shut off any exchange of information.

## Ancient China was better than the current "old people's nation"

**SHAKU**

I find there is a strong bias in Japan, especially in the pro-Chinese news coverages. For example, they describe the protest rally in Hong Kong as "a gathering of rioters" or that the movement has become "too radical and is very dangerous." But the truth is that the police are the "dangerous" ones there.

While such biased news reports exist in Japan, I think the influence of the younger generation disseminating correct information via Twitter and other social media, will definitely have a greater effect from now on.

Regarding the dissemination of information, we just heard that Xi Jinping's daughter plays a critical role in creating a "surveillance nation" in China. It is highly likely that these younger generations will clash against each other. What is your view on this?

**AGNES CHOW'S G.S.**

Well, Xi Jinping's daughter may have much power behind the scenes, but in my eyes China is already an "old people's nation." I can only see it as a gathering of people, who lived through the history of the Communist Party, banding together to consider matters and make decisions. I doubt that the opinion of the younger generation will affect anything. I can hardly believe their opinions will be taken seriously. While certain people are appointed to different administrative divisions, it is unlikely that these people can report negatively on China and make suggestions to the upper echelon of the Chinese government.

There was a Remonstrance Bureau even in Medieval China as a way to scrutinize policies and decisions, but in the current Xi Jinping system of governance, there is nobody who can remonstrate him.

While I don't really know about the daughter's involvement, in regards to the younger generation and their opinions, I doubt that they can have any public authority to do something officially.

### *"Overturn of the election ban is a ploy to look acceptable to other countries"*

**SHAKU**
After founding the political party, Demosisto, following the Umbrella Revolution, Ms. Agnes Chow attempted to run in the by-election and was banned. Yesterday (September 2), however, the Hong Kong High Court ruled that the election officer was unfair in imposing an election ban on Ms. Agnes Chow. As a result, there's a possibility for you to run for candidacy in the next election.

## AGNES CHOW'S G.S.

No, it's simply a "bait" and we need to be watchful of it. Even if they approve my running for candidacy and encourage me to voice our concerns, they could contain our power after electing me as a member of the legislative council. They could have such a plan.

If they are concerned about judgement from other countries, they could do that. There are plenty of ways to manipulate the results. For instance, they could manipulate the number of our voters to make it look smaller, or if they prefer to affect the political party as a whole, they could suppress our influence on people.

So far, it's hard for me to believe what they say, particularly because there is a possibility that they are trying to catch us off guard. It's quite possible for them to make empty promises of shifting into a more democratic form of governance. For now, it is more likely that they are trying to remove the problem at hand.

## AYAORI

In Hong Kong right now...

## AGNES CHOW'S G.S.

[*Pointing at the glass of water on the table.*] Excuse me, could you change this glass? I can't drink from the same glass that "(the guardian spirit of) Mr. Xi Jinping" drank out of. I'm sorry.

**AYAORI**
Ah, we're sorry.

**AGNES CHOW'S G.S.**
I just can't stand it, I can't.

**AYAORI**
One moment, please.

**AGNES CHOW'S G.S.**
[*Moving the glass to the right edge of the table.*] Put it away.
Here.

**AYAORI**
We're very sorry about this.

# 5

# The Points of Compromise in This Fight

## 1) First, make them withdraw the extradition bill

**AYAORI**
We would like to continue with the interview.

**AGNES CHOW'S G.S.**
Yes, sure.

**AYAORI**
From the perspectives of both China and the Western countries, what is currently happening in Hong Kong can be regarded as a "revolution"; China sees it as a revolution to overturn the government, while the West understands it as a revolution to found freedom. With this in mind, what do you think are the points of compromise, and what parts do you consider to be "victories?"

**AGNES CHOW'S G.S.**
First, we must clearly state that we will completely withdraw and abandon the extradition bill (extradition law amendments) eternally.

## 2) Resignation of the current Hong Kong Chief Executive, and creating a system to freely elect a successor

### AGNES CHOW'S G.S.

Since Chief Executive Carrie Lam is a puppet of the Chinese government, removing her doesn't make too much of a difference in reality... And if Beijing sends another Chief Executive, the situation would remain the same.

But still, I would like for her to resign and publicly admit to the faults in her decisions, which instigated much disorder in Hong Kong. Even for formalities sake, she needs to resign; otherwise it would be difficult to put an end to this matter.

And I would like China to recognize a free and fair voting procedure to elect the next Chief Executive, rather than have them make the selection for us.

## 3) Respect for human rights—guarantee "freedom of religion," "freedom of press" and other rights

### AGNES CHOW'S G.S.

And also the so-called "right to freedom." We need all kinds of basic human rights—"freedom of speech," "freedom of expression," "freedom of press," "freedom of religion," and "freedom from slave-like restrictions." We also need "freedom to fair trial." These kinds of freedom must be guaranteed and I want to demand these things from them.

## 4) If possible, we would like to see the independence of Hong Kong

### AGNES CHOW'S G.S.

If possible, I want to become a politician in the future to realize these things, but I know I lack the power to do so at the moment. My ultimate goal is to lead Hong Kong to independence, though it would be difficult without greater patronage.

### AYAORI

You're thinking as far as independence of Hong Kong?

### AGNES CHOW'S G.S.

Yes. I don't think we can win unless we think that far.

### SHAKU

So far, you have advocated to maintain the "One country, two systems" principle, and I thought you had taken a different stance from the pro-independence groups.

**AGNES CHOW'S G.S.**

I'm starting to despise being referred to as "Chinese." I associate myself more as being a "Hongkonger."

**SHAKU**

It seems like your stance has gradually been changing.

**AGNES CHOW'S G.S.**

The feeling that "We are Hongkongers, not Chinese" is becoming stronger. Yes. I think Taiwanese people should also distinguish themselves and say they are not Chinese, because if they accept to being Chinese, they will be absorbed.

**SHAKU**

I see.

**AYAORI**

Just a moment ago, you spoke of a need of greater patronage. When considering independence, do you think it would be difficult without external support?

**AGNES CHOW'S G.S.**

Well, it would be ideal to have the United States back us up, but in their current state, I am not sure whether there is enough room for them to handle the issue...

## 5) I want British Prime Minister Johnson to declare Hong Kong as part of the British Empire

**AGNES CHOW'S G.S.**

It would also be nice if England declared something like, "We would not hesitate to stand up and protect the people of Hong Kong," once again. I heard someone like Mr. Trump has appeared in England...

**AYAORI**

Are you talking about Prime Minister Johnson?

**AGNES CHOW'S G.S.**

I just think he's a bit different from the others.

**AYAORI**

Yes, that's right.

**AGNES CHOW'S G.S.**

I would be happy if he'd do something unexpected like that.

**AYAORI**

Oh, I see.

**AGNES CHOW'S G.S.**
Yes. I'd be happy if he'd say something like, "We are responsible for Hong Kong."

**AYAORI**
I see. In that sense, he could point out that China has breached the Sino-British Joint Declaration, which guaranteed Hong Kong's freedom for 50 years.

**AGNES CHOW'S G.S.**
At the very least, they've already broken their promise.

**AYAORI**
Right.

**AGNES CHOW'S G.S.**
Yes, Yes. Hong Kong was occupied by the United Kingdom as a result of the Opium War, so people were initially happy to return to China. In Hong Kong cinema, too, many anti-Japanese and anti-British movies were made. But now we are experiencing how bad life actually is to be a part of China. So was it Boris Johnson? The "Mr. Trump of England"?

**AYAORI**
Yes, that's right.

## AGNES CHOW'S G.S.

I think something very interesting would happen if he declared to occupy Hong Kong once again.

## AYAORI

I see. So you mean Hong Kong will return to the jurisdiction of Britain.

## AGNES CHOW'S G.S.

Yes. Well actually, rather than "returning to the jurisdiction," if he said something like, "We will re-occupy Hong Kong, unless you recognize Hong Kong's autonomy and independence," and sent a warship over, it would be interesting. Since he is new, nobody really knows what kind of person he is, so I bet China would be fearful. Especially since they have no idea what "British Trump" might do.

## AYAORI

Oh, I see. Yes. It is unpredictable.

## AGNES CHOW'S G.S.

It would be great if he would commit to protecting the British Empire and include Hong Kong under the same umbrella as the other countries of the British Empire, like Australia and Canada.

**AYAORI**

As you say, Britain might start moving toward rebuild-ing its empire after leaving the EU and returning to its original ways.

**AGNES CHOW'S G.S.**

Yes, yes. That's right. I think they would be lonely, so it's better to have more allies. Don't you think so? I think they should unilaterally declare that they recognize Hong Kong as part of the British Empire at 10 Downing Street.

**AYAORI**

Yes. I see. That would send a very clear message.

**AGNES CHOW'S G.S.**

It's interesting. Even if we don't have a war, just by making that statement, I bet that Xi Jinping would get cold feet. It would be interesting.

**AYAORI**

I see.

# 6

## Thinking as Far as the Democratization of China

### *Realizing Mao Zedong's revolution and Deng Xiaoping's reforms were a sham*

**FUJII**
As I listen to you talk, I sense a very strategic perspective from you.

**AGNES CHOW'S G.S.**
Thank you.

**FUJII**
Do you ever feel like your sense of mission deepens as you continue with your activities?

**AGNES CHOW'S G.S.**
I've been arrested before and I feel there is no turning back after having come this far. I've realized very clearly that Mao Zedong's revolution was a sham. And furthermore, it became clear to me that the theoretical system of "socialism with Chinese characteristics," used by Deng Xiaoping as a way to separate economy and politics, was also fake. Even though he disseminated fantasies that China would become a leading world power with this "socialist

market economy" and would prevent going down the same road as the Soviet Union, I realized this system essentially doesn't take into account the happiness of the people and is therefore a mistake that should not be spread.

What we are experiencing now is the result of failing to put an end to this injustice during the Tiananmen Square incident. Even though the incident was before my time, I believe that western and international societies should have sent an investigation committee to reveal the truth and solved the issue properly, but they didn't; rather, they let their rule prolonged, which led to the current situation. It is unclear if we will witness more casualties in Hong Kong, but I'm sure any result will be more visible and accessible to the international countries than it was during the Tiananmen Square protests. Yes.

**AYAORI**
According to the spiritual message received from Xi Jinping's guardian spirit just a moment ago, he spoke of the possibility of suppressing activities using military power, as a way to "cleanse."

**AGNES CHOW'S G.S.**
Cleansing? Cleansing is important. Cleansing is important.

**AYAORI**

Yes.

**AGNES CHOW'S G.S.**

Yes. Cleansing is important.

**AYAORI**

They mean "cleansing" from a Chinese perspective.

**AGNES CHOW'S G.S.**

In that case, they should "cleanse" Zhongnanhai.

**AYAORI**

Yes, you have a point.

**AGNES CHOW'S G.S.**

Yes.

## The true meaning behind "the need for extreme measures"

**AYAORI**

At a time when military suppression is a real possibility, Ms. Agnes Chow commented in an interview about "the need to take extreme measures," which we think this is very foresightful. What do you think she means by this?

## AGNES CHOW'S G.S.

China wants to suppress people in Hong Kong so much that they send members of the People's Liberation Army to secretly join the Hong Kong police. This being so, we must resist to some extent.

## AYAORI

Hmm.

## AGNES CHOW'S G.S.

As you implied earlier, we mostly don't have any real weapons. What we are doing is no more than creating barricades by taking apart iron fences and removing bolts and nuts. That's all we can do.

If China really decides to send armed forces to suppress us, we would need more "patronage" like I mentioned earlier. We would be grateful if there are other countries who are willing to supply us with resources, such as food, energy, and vehicles, so we can resist to some extent. I am trying to reach out to people around the world with that hope. I wish there were a country with such views of noblesse oblige.

## *Xi Jinping has the decisive power to turn Hong Kong into a concentration camp and to realize "modern Nazism"*

### AGNES CHOW'S G.S.

It seems like the Japanese government is not only going to ignore South Korea now, but also Hong Kong entirely. It's unfortunate that the voice from the Happiness Realization Party has not reached far enough.

### SHAKU

We're sorry.

### AGNES CHOW'S G.S.

It's frustrating.

### SHAKU

While we stand in a very frustrating situation, we believe we are the only people who are capable of spreading the correct understanding within Japan.

With Xi Jinping staying put, Hong Kong is at the forefront of the battle against communism. If Hong Kong falls, next will be Taiwan. Then Okinawa, Senkaku Islands, Japan, and the South China Sea. Chairman Xi Jinping has a similar understanding of this and is determined not to budge an inch.

## AGNES CHOW'S G.S.

Hmm.

## SHAKU

Since there is a chance that this clash will occur before October 1, I understand the current situation is extremely tense. How do you plan to overcome this situation?

## AGNES CHOW'S G.S.

If Xi Jinping truly decides that it's inevitable for people in Hong Kong to be annihilated, no matter how much international criticism he receives, he will unify the country and will not tolerate any form of rebellion.

He's already taken over Tibet entirely, and the Xinjiang Uyghur Autonomous Region has been turned into a concentration camp. This already is "modern Nazism." He is enforcing such terrors without hesitation, without a care about international criticism.

Given these circumstances, I think he would want to put Hong Kong inside the iron fences in its entirety and turn it into one big concentration camp.

## SHAKU

But there are about 20,000 Japanese residents in Hong Kong.

**AGNES CHOW'S G.S.**

Japanese people can escape.

**SHAKU**

That's true. If Hong Kong were to face such conditions, other countries around the world would certainly condemn China and impose economic sanctions. I think there is more we can do from overseas to pressure China, and...

**AGNES CHOW'S G.S.**

Well, that's exactly what China has been trying to prevent. It has strategically built close relationships with other countries through projects like the One Belt, One Road Initiative and created a situation in which imposing economic sanctions on China would trigger a global financial crisis. In this regard, they are cunning and strategic.

**SHAKU**

It seems we are entering a time where President Trump's greatness becomes evident.

**AGNES CHOW'S G.S.**

But China's strategy has progressed so far that an economic sanction from the United States, just one country, is not effective, so this is a very tough situation.

## *Japan contributed too much to China's economic growth and amplified its development by dozens of times*

**FUJII**

If you have a big plan, we are hoping you'd depend on Happy Science to be of assistance in carrying it out.

**AGNES CHOW'S G.S.**

Hmm.

**FUJII**

We understand you are thinking as far as independence of Hong Kong. We assume you are the guiding spirit of Ms. Agnes Chow, and we are curious about how Ms. Agnes Chow viewed the Tiananmen Square incident from the Spirit World before being born...

**AGNES CHOW'S G.S.**

Very frustrated.

**FUJII**

How do you think of your mission in this lifetime? Is it to somehow change China?

**AGNES CHOW'S G.S.**

All evil must be condemned clearly. Mr. Xi Jinping is probably thinking that it is OK for Hong Kong to become run-down as long as mainland China flourishes from absorbing Hong Kong's financial center and its other functions. He will probably insert people from China and do away with the Hongkongers by dispersing them to various concentration camps in different locations so that the act remains undetected by the international community. In this way, they've already abandoned Hong Kong's prosperity.

Taiwan may not be able to speak up as much as they'd like because of the fear of an expedited attack from China as a result.

In regards to Japan, I believe they have contributed too much to the development of the Chinese economy. By building factories and employing many Chinese workers, Japan has helped amplify China's development by dozens of times. The United States may have helped a little as well, but the influence of Japanese corporations is significant. Only in recent times, have they finally started loaning and moving their factories to pro-Japanese locations like Africa.

China has reclaimed a military base from the ocean and has established a system in which other Southeast Asian countries, like the Philippines and Vietnam, are within missile range. There is a high chance they will use the military forces to take control of those areas.

## "I want to involve southern cities like Shenzhen as we lead Hong Kong to independence"

**AYAORI**

You mentioned the independence of Hong Kong, but how do you view the democratization of mainland China?

**AGNES CHOW'S G.S.**

Ah, I want to make it happen. I've thought as far as that. While Mr. Xi Jinping is actually trying to move Hong Kong's functions to places like Shenzhen, my hope is to lead Hong Kong to independence while also involving places like Shenzhen in the process. I'd like to recreate something similar to the state of Wu in the Three Kingdoms period.

**SHAKU**

I see.

**AGNES CHOW'S G.S.**

People who prefer socialism can continue living in the north, but we dislike the system, and I believe some people in the south also want to become independent. I think it would be OK for people who want to become independent from China to join us in that free country.

**AYAORI**
There is a slightly similar air to the Taiping Rebellion.

**AGNES CHOW'S G.S.**
Our movement could be like that. It's possible.

**SHAKU**
I actually saw some younger women in their twenties in Hong Kong who were using the terms "Northern people" and "Southern people," and referring to themselves as "Southern people."

**AGNES CHOW'S G.S.**
Hmm.

**SHAKU**
I understand this new self-awareness is spreading more and more.

**AGNES CHOW'S G.S.**
It's definitely true. I'm having trouble graduating university because I don't really want to speak Mandarin. Hahaha. I'm not good at Standard Chinese.

# 7

## The Spirits that Agnes Chow's Guardian Spirit Interacts with in the Spirit World

### *Receiving guidance from the philosopher, Hannah Arendt*

**AYAORI**

Switching over to a more spiritual topic, what kind of spiritual being do you speak to normally when you are in a situation like the current state? In other words, what kind of spirit is your advisor?

**AGNES CHOW'S G.S.**

Hahaha. I'm not that accomplished...

**AYAORI**

That's not true.

**AGNES CHOW'S G.S.**

I'm only 22 years old.

**FUJII**

You have a very international perspective.

## AGNES CHOW'S G.S.

Hehe. I don't think I do. I mostly study by watching Japanese anime, so I doubt that I do.

## AYAORI

In our last spiritual interview with you, we recorded a very short conversation in which a philosopher named Hannah Arendt was mentioned.

## AGNES CHOW'S G.S.

Ah, yes. I am certainly receiving guidance from the spirit of Dr. Arendt[*].

## *"You should conduct spiritual research on Shiro Amakusa, a Japanese revolutionary, as well"*

## AYAORI

I'm sure this is true for you now, but in a time when action is wanted, I presume you may also be receiving a different kind of guidance.

---

[*] On the day after this interview was recorded, another spiritual interview, "Spiritual Messages from Hannah Arendt," was recorded. See Chapter 4.

## AGNES CHOW'S G.S.

It seems like other powers and certain religious powers are getting involved as well.

## AYAORI

Are you talking about some guidance from Christian-related spirits?

## AGNES CHOW'S G.S.

Christianity and Judaism... and I feel some other religions are also involved.

## SHAKU

When I witnessed a gathering at a stadium of people waving their hands back and forth as they all sang a hymn, "Sing Hallelujah to the Lord," I was so moved it brought tears to my eyes. I felt a sense of love and peace and solidarity in this wonderful atmosphere, and it was clear to me that this movement was receiving support from God.

## AGNES CHOW'S G.S.

That's right. Are you familiar with Shiro Amakusa*? I know of a famous Japanese singer regarding himself as having such a past life.

**SHAKU**

Oh.

**AGNES CHOW'S G.S.**

See?

**SHAKU**

Yes.

**AGNES CHOW'S G.S.**

Hehe. It'd be good to do a spiritual interview with him.[†]

**AYAORI**

Ohh. I wonder if you have some connection with him.

**AGNES CHOW'S G.S.**

Perhaps, yes.

---

[*] Shiro Amakusa (1621?-1639) Christian leader who led the Shimabara Rebellion. This rebellion occurred due to the oppression and heavy taxation of Christians by the Shimabara domain in 1637. At the age of 16, he became the leader of the rebellion and fought for 90 days to protect the Hara Castle in the Shimabara peninsula in Nagasaki. It was the largest revolt in Japanese history but was ultimately suppressed. The statue of Shiro Amakusa stands on the hillside of the Shiro Amakusa Park.

[†] On the day after this interview was recorded, another spiritual interview, "Spiritual Messages from Shiro Amakusa," was recorded. See Chapter 3.

**AYAORI**

Is it possible that you are himself?

**AGNES CHOW'S G.S.**

Well, you see, I can speak Japanese.

**AYAORI**

Ah, I see what you mean.

**AGNES CHOW'S G.S.**

Yes.

**AYAORI**

I see. So, this must be a true religious battle.

**AGNES CHOW'S G.S.**

Yes. So, it is possible that we will be suppressed. If Shiro Amakusa had won the Shimabara Rebellion, Japan could have become a Christian country and may have joined the other Western countries.

**AYAORI**

Ohh.

## *"How do I want to die? I suppose on a cross?"*

### SHAKU

When I visited Hong Kong, I saw people of various religious backgrounds contributing to the movement. Not only were there Christians but also an anti-communist party group called Falun Gong distributing newspapers or flyers, and I heard Buddhists and people of various religious backgrounds saying, "We are participating in this movement with religious faith as our motivator." Are you aware, or do you have a sense of mission that you were born bearing the large tide of the world?

### AGNES CHOW'S G.S.

In recent years, such religious powers are starting to work, so I don't know how much I could contribute to it. I heard Xi Jinping's guardian spirit just brought up the topic of how I'd want to die. Well, I wonder how... I suppose on a cross? I'm not sure.

In regards to man-power, it is a battle of 1.4 billion versus 7 million, so China has the power to annihilate us completely. It can be done with a single decision by one person.

## *Mr. Trump's unique negotiation tactics is likely to send China the wrong message*

### AGNES CHOW'S G.S.

I think Mr. Trump's negotiation tactics are unique. For instance, when he met Kim Jong-Un, Mr. Trump would try and flatter him by saying he is smart or that he is trustworthy and that he has kept his promises. But those kinds of comments might give China the wrong impression. While this might be normal in American business settings, in dealing with China and North Korea, I think Mr. Trump needs to be more clear about his intentions.

Right now, it looks as if the United States is fighting China just over tariffs, and if the United States continues to send positive "signals" to North Korea, people may mistakenly believe the United States doesn't want to fight China.

### AYAORI

I believe his stance is slowly changing, though.

## *The spirits of revolutionaries who give advice in the Spirit World*

### AYAORI

Excuse me. I believe you mostly receive guidance from a

Christian spirit, but would you tell us who specifically you are receiving advice from?

## AGNES CHOW'S G.S.
Well, I don't know if it's a good idea to reveal their names.

## AYAORI
Oh, really.

## AGNES CHOW'S G.S.
Um, there is certainly someone who tried to reform the Qing dynasty a long time ago.

## AYAORI
I'm assuming they were Christians.

## AGNES CHOW'S G.S.
I don't know if they were Christian. It might be better to call it a "new religion."

## AYAORI
Oh, you are speaking of the other person. You mean the revolutionary of the Qing dynasty?

**AGNES CHOW'S G.S.**

If they had succeeded, a Meiji Restoration-like incident might have occurred in Qing.

**AYAORI**

I suppose it's Hong Xiuquan*, right?

**AGNES CHOW'S G.S.**

Yes. Spirits like him often visit me. They are here for support, but they've all lost their fights, so perhaps odds are still against us. There are spirits from Japan as well.

**AYAORI**

Ahh, is that so?

**AGNES CHOW'S G.S.**

They come to give some support.

**AYAORI**

Are they spirits involved in the Meiji Restoration?

---

* Hong Xiuquan (1814-1864) was the leader of the Taiping Heavenly Kingdom in the Qing Dynasty of China. After failing the imperial examination many times, he formed the God Worshipping Society. He fought the Qing army in the Taiping Revolution but lost, and would later die from illness.

**AGNES CHOW'S G.S.**
They don't come very often, but I sometimes receive guidance from spirits that claim themselves to be Mr. Ryoma Sakamoto and Mr. Shinsaku Takasugi[*].

**AYAORI**
Oh, they're central figures during that time.

**AGNES CHOW'S G.S.**
They come to cheer me on.

**SHAKU**
Mr. Shinsaku Takasugi also started a revolution when he saw the situation of the Qing dynasty from Shanghai.

**AGNES CHOW'S G.S.**
That's why he is cheering me on, but in order to fight, we need "fuel," and I am not sure if Japan will actually take some action in support of that...

---

[*] Ryoma Sakamoto (1835-1867), Shinsaku Takasugi (1839-1867) were prominent samurai leaders of the Meiji Restoration.

## *"Be water"—Bruce Lee's words based on Taoism*

**AYAORI**
The quote, "Be water" is becoming a slogan of the Hong Kong protests.

**SHAKU**
"Be water."

**AGNES CHOW'S G.S.**
Yes.

**AYAORI**
Given that this phrase was often used by Bruce Lee, would you say he is providing strong support as well?

**AGNES CHOW'S G.S.**
Well, we do need a hero. I guess Hong Kong has a bronze statue of him. Putting Bruce Lee aside, those in the stream of Lao Tzu philosophy for example... well, they also despise oppressive rule. Taoist philosophy still underlies Chinese philosophy. Even the Communist Party conducts funerals with Taoist rites, so they cannot eradicate Taoist influences completely. Indeed, there is also some support from Taoists that preach the "teachings of water."

# 8

# To the Youth Around the World—
# "This is a Revolution,"
# "Now is the Time to Fight"

## *"Those who can see the Truth must be strong despite small numbers"*

**SHAKU**

To close our interview, it would be great if we could ask for your message to the people of the younger generation in Japan and all around the world. As we are strongly moved by Ms. Agnes Chow's extremely pure motivation, we would love to hear a message from you addressing the youth.

**AGNES CHOW'S G.S.**

Even though the opponent may seem tremendously big, if you look at it from a different angle, they are all "blinded." Though they are 1.4 billion in number, they all have blinders on. I believe those who can see the Truth must be strong, no matter how small in number. So, "courage" should be our slogan and "overcoming fear" is vital.

## WWII escalated because the fight against the Nazis were delayed

### AGNES CHOW'S G.S.

People may say that there is no chance of our victory and fighting against Greater China will only lead to a tragic result.

But when Nazi Germany began their "hunt" for Jewish people, even though churches gave shelter to some of the Jews, Britain and France avoided war with an appeasement policy. That resulted in expanding the battlefront and allowing World War II to become colossal. I think they should have perceived the Nazis as evil at an early stage and deterred its expansion immediately. Finally, toward the end of the war, Winston Churchill fought back believing "Hitler is the Devil" and decided he will never surrender. This may have reaped good results in the end, but it was actually too late to take action; it should have been done at a much earlier stage.

In our current situation, I believe Master Ryuho Okawa is trying to crush the "One Belt, One Road" Initiative, and Japan is being influenced by his philosophy. Even though Mr. Abe has not been able to reach a successful negotiation with Russia, it is crucial to get both Russia and the United States involved in thwarting China's ambition now. If China successfully takes control over Africa and Europe, they will be unstoppable. The world will become a surveillance society, and personal freedom and basic human rights will be taken away.

In the end, the reason why such things can happen is the lack of faith in God. Atheism and materialism will only look at an individual as a cogwheel and judge people based on their utility to the greater system. Unless we take action at an early stage to fight such nation that views people in this way, there is a chance our enemy will continue to gain power.

### *"We may die, but it will not be in vain"*

**AGNES CHOW'S G.S.**

We may die, but we also believe it will not be in vain. If we don't fight now, something tragic is bound to happen in Taiwan next. If something happens to Taiwan, various incidents will start to occur in many other places including the South China Sea. The domination of Asia will begin from various bombing and missile bases that China has been constructing in recent years. There is no doubt that Xi Jinping, who is president for life, will do the same thing Hitler did.

Mr. Trump will eventually step down from office, so we need to establish a regime that can counter such move. To do this, the current Abe administration is not enough, so we had truly hoped the Happiness Realization Party to have gained some seats in the central government.

But I suppose Japan has been failing to succeed in this revolution for 10 years.

Even though we may die in this fight, if our deaths provoke the surrounding countries and other countries around the world to believe that justice lies in preserving democracy that protects basic human rights and faith in God, we believe our deaths would not go to waste. That is why we will continue to fight, knowing that one or two thousand lives, or even ten thousand of them, might be sacrificed in the process.

I hope Japan will move past our death and carry on our efforts by changing their national policy and making Japan a country that can speak up about what is right. Please stop being so submissive to a greater or stronger power all the time, but become a nation that can speak its mind.

## *"Please send Japan's Self-Defense Forces and the U.S. and British armies to Hong Kong"*

### AGNES CHOW'S G.S.

If possible, I would like Japan's Self-Defense Forces to be sent to Hong Kong. Please send Self-Defense Forces. That is my true wish. However, I doubt this is possible with the current Japanese administration. They won't even meet with me, so I don't think they have the guts.

There are 20,000 Japanese nationals living in Hong Kong, and the Japanese government will probably only think of evacuating them. They will only be concerned about sending their citizens back to Japan, but if there are 20,000 of them, I hope they would dispatch Self-Defense Forces under the pretext of protecting their citizens.

If they do, the United States will also make a move. They definitely will. If Japan just waits for the United States to make the first move, no move would likely arise in the world to support us.

I don't know how many people will read this book, but please send Self-Defense Forces to Hong Kong under the pretext of protecting Japanese nationals. If that happens, the U.S. Army will definitely come, too. Please also encourage Prime Minister Boris Johnson to send his troops by saying that the "British Empire" still has unfinished duties. With the American, British, and Japanese forces on our side, we will be able to continue fighting. But if everyone looks the other way, we will be crushed and Taiwan will be next.

### *"Now is the time to fight"—This is a revolution for independence*

**AGNES CHOW'S G.S.**

I believe now is the time to fight. How long I live is now up to Xi Jinping. If his intentions of "cleansing" by October 1 includes my death, I'm sure they have come up with about a hundred different ways to kill me by now. Making accidents happen is easy for them. They could make a crane truck suddenly swing around to kill me. Or they could kill me in an unexpected fire, in a made-up internal division or strife, or in an accidental crossfire between the police forces. I'm sure they have researched all possibilities and the consequences as well.

However, we are already prepared to lose a thousand, two thousand, even ten thousand lives. This is a revolution. We intend to lead Hong Kong toward independence eventually. We are counting on everyone in Japan for support.

## AYAORI
Thank you very much. We will continue to fight as much as possible in the coming month.

## *"Let God's glory shine on Earth while I am still alive"*

## AGNES CHOW'S G.S.
I think Japan must learn to make decisions and take action more quickly. It shouldn't be only passively observing the situation.

As you can see from his earlier spiritual interview, Xi Jinping really does not care about the happiness of people. His goal is to become the world's most powerful person. But I don't think this should be allowed.

Please let God's glory shine on Earth while I am still alive, if possible. I ask you.

There are many spirits supporting us, but those in the Spirit World do not have the worldly powers. We can be killed with a single bullet, and it may be impossible to prevent it from happening altogether. If China decides to send troops to Hong Kong, it is highly likely for most of the main activists to be killed or imprisoned within three days, because there is nowhere to hide in Hong Kong. They will be able to have control over every corner of the region.

I have little hope for Japan's Self-Defense Forces to be sent... but still, I ask this of you. Please come and help us. Please.

**SHAKU**
We understand.

**AYAORI**
Thank you very much.

### *"I'm counting on the Happy Science branch working hard in Hong Kong"*

**AGNES CHOW'S G.S.**
Ah, the Happy Science branch in Hong Kong is also working very hard. They seem to suggest we should rely on

them and say, "Please run into this Happy Science branch in times of need," so I count on them a bit. But as long as you are located in Hong Kong, it would be a piece of cake for People's Liberation Army to destroy a small city state like us, if they were to intervene; they have a power to take over a whole country.

Even so, we will fight as much as we can. I pray for more people in Japan to have such feelings.

**SHAKU**
We will do everything we can, with all our might.

**AGNES CHOW'S G.S.**
Yes. Thank you very much.

# 9

## After the Spiritual Interview: As a State of Emergency Approaches, Japan Must Make Quick Decisions and Take Action

### *There is no way of stopping Xi Jinping taking a hard line without a joint resolution between Japan, the United States, Britain, and the EU*

### RYUHO OKAWA

[*Claps twice.*] Well, I'm not sure if a tragedy will strike, but Xi Jinping will not be able to dominate Taiwan if he fails in solving this matter. So, it is no surprise that he will end up taking a hard line, whether he will take majority vote or decide on his own as a dictator. To prevent that, the United States, Britain, Japan, and the EU must decide to support Hong Kong; otherwise, he will most likely be unstoppable.

On the other hand, if Hong Kong were to be successfully protected, then it will open up a way for Xinjiang Uyghur, Tibet, and Inner Mongolia Autonomous Regions and provoke movements for independence in various locations. This is probably what Xi Jinping fears the most.

## *Without a sense of righteousness, no governance is just*

### RYUHO OKAWA

"Maintenance of peace is the most important component of governance" is one way of thinking, but what really needs consideration is the idea that "Without a sense of righteousness, we cannot say a governance is just." This is a matter of what justice is. It is now imperative that we spread the teachings of Happy Science as widely as possible.

At the same time, since there seems to be a significant number of people planning to emigrate from Hong Kong, Japan also needs to prepare by creating enough room to accept such people. While the Japanese government will likely be slow in making decisions, it is important to do what we can.

## *Japan must hastily prepare by simulating a potential state of emergency in Hong Kong and Korea*

### RYUHO OKAWA

While I don't want anyone to die, the next target will most definitely be Taiwan, followed by Okinawa.

South Korean President Moon Jae-in seems to be acting oddly recently; after having decided to scrap the General Security of Military Information Agreement (GSOMIA) with Japan, he is now looking to create new ties with Thailand. I have no idea what he intends to accomplish by this new agreement and what will be made possible by exchanging military information with Thailand. It only seems like he is confused and is slowly losing his mind.

There is a potential escalation of conflicts in both Hong Kong and the Korean Peninsula, so by now Japan must simulate and be ready to make quick decisions and to act accordingly. Otherwise, Japan will face danger.

At this point in time, I can only take action in this prophetic way, but perhaps it is better than no action. It seems like Prime Minister Abe and his associates have nowhere else to depend on but Happy Science, so I believe I must say what needs to be said.

## Even though isolationism does not guarantee safety, the Japanese media alters the point of issue to maintain the status quo

### RYUHO OKAWA

I definitely want the Happiness Realization Party to win some seats in the next national election. Since the Japanese media has strong leftist views, they have the tendency to change the point of issue just for the sake of maintaining the status quo, making it harder for us to win. There are many incidents occurring abroad, so I wish they'd change their ways of thinking even a bit. Basically they still hold the idea of "isolationism" and believe that peace in their own country is all that matters. In our current state, however, we cannot assume that the ocean would protect us from any invasions.

The guardian spirit of President Moon once said in a spiritual interview that it is possible for the South and North Koreas to unite and form a regime to attack Japan. Considering that comment, it may be dangerous to assume that Japan is safe simply because it is surrounded by the ocean and is therefore "isolated." We should be the ones upholding the "Juche (self-reliance) ideology." We need to persevere and keep trying.

## AYAORI

Yes. We will continue to try our best.

## Politics, media, citizens, and Happy Science were too slow to act

## RYUHO OKAWA

I've introduced the opinions of the guardian spirits of both Mr. Xi Jinping and Ms. Agnes Chow. But even if we publish this, I suppose only 10,000 to 20,000 books are sold in the end.

## AYAORI

No, we will definitely try to use various methods to spread our messages more widely.

## RYUHO OKAWA

The influence of this book will be very limited since only about 1,000 to 2,000 people who are non-members of Happy Science will probably read this book.

## SHAKU

We will make sure to spread it widely.

## RYUHO OKAWA

Internationally, there are probably only about 100 to 200 copies printed and distributed on demand.

## AYAORI

We will make sure to inform the central governments of Japan and the United States as well.

## RYUHO OKAWA

We lacked power and speed; perhaps our move was too slow. The Japanese public offices, government, mass media, and citizens are all too slow. This is truly a tough situation.

### *Japan needs more people who can confidently speak up*

## RYUHO OKAWA

A Japanese member of the House of Representatives, Hodaka Maruyama, known for bringing up the possibility of war in a discussion about the Northern Islands, recently changed his party and now belongs to the "Party to Protect the People from NHK." He then spoke of war as the only option regarding Takeshima Island, and this was again accused by the media. They cannot see what is important.

The other day, leftist media reported that the South Korean National Assembly member stepped foot on Shimane Prefecture's Takeshima Island. If Japan truly claims Takeshima to be their land, they should not simply respond to the news as being "regrettable" but understand it as an "invasion of territory" and send the Self-Defense Forces. However, this is apparently prohibited.

There are some truly confusing areas about the thinking processes of this country, and I really think Japan needs more people who can confidently speak up. Anyway, let us continue our efforts.

## ALL INTERVIEWERS
Yes. Thank you very much.

## RYUHO OKAWA
Thank you.

# Chapter Three

# Spiritual Messages from Shiro Amakusa

Recorded September 4, 2019
Special Lecture Hall, Happy Science,
Japan

# Shiro Tokisada Amakusa (1621? - 1638)

A Japanese Christian leader of the early Edo period. His real name was Masuda Shiro Tokisada. After returning to Amakusa from his studies in Nagasaki, he performed many miracles and was said to be the second coming of the Child of God prophesied by Father Marco Ferraro. In 1637, he became the leader of the Shimabara Rebellion to fight against the heavy taxation, oppression, and persecution of Christians. He took over the Hara Castle on Shimabara Island, but fell in 90 days. The rebel force was annihilated.

Interviewers from Happy Science[*]:

Shio Okawa
Aide to Master

Sakurako Jinmu
Managing Director
Chief Secretary of First Secretarial Division
Religious Affairs Headquarters

*The opinions of the spirit do not necessarily reflect those of Happy Science Group. For the mechanism behind spiritual messages, see end section.*

---

[*] Interviewers are listed in the order that they appear in the transcript.
Their professional titles represent their positions at the time of the interview.

# 1

## His Spiritual Connection with the Soul of Jesus Christ

### What's happening in Hong Kong is a battle between an atheist nation and religious forces

**RYUHO OKAWA**

[*Takes a deep breath.*] Shiro Amakusa of Kyushu, who was born in the early Tokugawa era and instigated the people to spread Christianity in Japan. Shiro Amakusa, who revolted against the Tokugawa government but was suppressed by them.

Please come down to Happy Science and reveal to us your thoughts. The spirit of Shiro Amakusa, the spirit of Shiro Amakusa, the spirit of Shiro Amakusa... The spirit of Shiro Amakusa, the spirit of Shiro Amakusa.

[*About 10 seconds of silence.*]

**SHIRO AMAKUSA**

[*In a singing tone.*] Umm. Um. Um. Um. Um. Um. Um. U...m. Uh, uh, uh, uh, wu, wu, wu, wu. Umm, umm. Ah, um, um, um. Uh, wu, wu, wu, uhhm, umm, uhhm. Um. Um, umm. Um. Um. U...m. Ah... Ha... Umm. Um. Um.

Um. Ah, ha. Ha. Ha. Huh...n, huh...n. Ha, huh, huh...n.
Hu... hu... hu...n.

**RYUHO OKAWA**
He seems to be singing a song.

**SHIO OKAWA**
Is it a hymn?

**RYUHO OKAWA**
It sounds like a hymn.

**AMAKUSA**
Ho... Ho... Ho... Hong Kong... people... It may be tough...
but hang in there.... Ho, ho, ho... Oh, oh... Oh... Oh...

**SAKURAKO JINMU**
Hello.

**AMAKUSA**
He...llo...

**JINMU**
Are you Shiro Amakusa?

**AMAKUSA**

Oh, ye...s, I think I may... be... I do not know why but I start singing... I wonder why...

**JINMU**

What were you singing at the beginning?

**AMAKUSA**

Hmmm... a hymn... Perhaps?

**SHIO OKAWA**

Was it a song for Jesus?

**AMAKUSA**

Hmm... hmm... that's... right. Hmm, hymns are so nice. They are singing a hymn in Hong Kong. We can hear it in Heaven.

**SHIO OKAWA**

I see.

**AMAKUSA**

All of you in Hong Kong, we are watching you from Heaven, too.

**SHIO OKAWA**

You led the Shimabara Rebellion...

**AMAKUSA**

Yes.

**SHIO OKAWA**

At that time, Christian activities were suppressed in Japan.

**AMAKUSA**

In Hong Kong too, Christianity is taking the lead. Since it was under British rule, Christianity is most certainly taking the lead.

**SHIO OKAWA**

Yes.

**AMAKUSA**

So, this is a battle between an atheistic, materialistic nation and religious forces led by Christianity.

### The spiritual connection between Jesus and Shiro Amakusa, and the spiritual connection between Jesus and Agnes Chow

**SHIO OKAWA**

Yesterday (September 3, 2019), we talked with the guardian spirit of Ms. Agnes Chow Ting, who is known as Hong Kong's "Goddess of Democracy." (See Chapter 2.)

**AMAKUSA**

Yes, yes, yes.

**SHIO OKAWA**

At that time, she mentioned your name, Shiro Amakusa. What kind of connection do you have with Ms. Agnes Chow?

**AMAKUSA**

Hmm... We do have a connection.

**SHIO OKAWA**

What kind of connection?

**AMAKUSA**

I am mainly a religious figure, but I like democratic religious movements involving political activities...

**SHIO OKAWA**

Yes.

**AMAKUSA**

I also have interest in faith, prayer, and of course, healing illnesses and performing miracles as well. I am the type of soul that can work certain miracles.

**SHIO OKAWA**

I see.

**AMAKUSA**

Yes. In a broad sense, there are satellite souls that make up the soul of Jesus Christ.

**SHIO OKAWA**

Yes, yes.

**AMAKUSA**

John Lennon[*] is fairly close (to Jesus), and there are many souls who were burned to death during religious reforms.

**SHIO OKAWA**

Yes.

**AMAKUSA**

Most of those souls are my acquaintances.

**SHIO OKAWA**

Your acquaintances?

**AMAKUSA**

Yes.

---

[*] In January 2019, Happy Science recorded the spiritual messages from John Lennon three times. He revealed that his soul is a part of the Jesus Christ consciousness.

## SHIO OKAWA
What is your connection to Jesus?

## AMAKUSA
Jesus is my parent soul.

## SHIO OKAWA
I see. Yes, OK.

## AMAKUSA
Jesus is my parent soul. There are branch spirits that work as much as Jesus, but there are also those who have not reached that level. They are...

## SHIO OKAWA
Fragments?

## AMAKUSA
There are spirits that split off from the core spirit.

## JINMU
Like Oscar Wilde*?

---

* See *Spiritual Messages from Oscar Wilde: Love, Beauty, and LGBT* (Tokyo: HS Press, 2019).

**AMAKUSA**

Yes, yes. Like him.

**SHIO OKAWA**

He is "a piece of Jesus Christ."

**AMAKUSA**

Hmm. But I don't think even John Lennon can get as close to the core spirit of Jesus.

**SHIO OKAWA**

I see.

**AMAKUSA**

Oscar Wilde also said something like that, but there are many historical figures with the fragments of Jesus' soul in them. They have pieces of his soul in them.

# 2

# The "Ifs" in Japanese History: Nobunaga Oda and Modernization

## *"I was born with a mission to spread Christianity in Japan"*

### SHIO OKAWA

So, does that mean you received guidance from Jesus, but at the same time, you are close to him as a soul, and you were sort of created from his soul?

### AMAKUSA

I was born with a mission to spread Christianity to Japan.

### SHIO OKAWA

I see.

### AMAKUSA

That is why people like Francis Xavier (1506-1552) came to Japan as a Christian missionary and produced Christian believers in the Kyushu region of Japan. Perhaps, there were more Christians back then than there are now.

Although Christianity became popular, it was suppressed and barred politically, after all. The government did so using military force. If it weren't for them, I believe

Christianity would have spread more. The Tokugawa government adopted Confucianism and "Chinalized" Japan. In other words, they sort of brought Japan under Chinese rule.

## SHIO OKAWA

I see.

## *Japan had a chance to be modernized during the Nobunaga era*

## AMAKUSA

As a result, Japan grew stagnant, causing a delay of modernization until the Meiji Restoration. Japan had a chance to be modernized during Nobunaga's* rule, way before the Meiji Restoration. Had Japan adopted Christianity then, Japan would have been Westernized for sure. So, the modernization was delayed for about 300 to 400 years. Hmm...

## SHIO OKAWA

This topic came up in other spiritual messages, too.

---

* Nobunaga Oda (1534-1582) was a Japanese general who contributed the most to ending the Warring States Period and starting the modern era.

## JINMU

Perhaps it was (the guardian spirit of) Imam Khamenei.*

## AMAKUSA

Ah, OK. From the time of Nobunaga's rule, Japan had a chance to modernize itself. Modern Europe had already began around that time, and Japan could have joined that trend. But it (Christianity) was persecuted. So...

## SHIO OKAWA

When you were alive, what was the main issue in Japan that you fought against?

## AMAKUSA

Well, I believe that it is the same issue that Hong Kong is fighting against now: unification and stability of order.

## SHIO OKAWA

I see. Unification and stability of order may come, but in return, the happiness of individuals will wane...

## AMAKUSA

So, they value sustaining the government, which basically means being blessed with the heir to the shogun, right?

---

* In the spiritual message from the guardian spirit of Iranian Supreme Leader Khamenei, conducted on June 17, 2019, he said that Japan came under the influence of China when the Tokugawa government adopted Confucianism.

**SHIO OKAWA**
Yes.

**AMAKUSA**
Just like the current imperial family in Japan. It's important for them to be blessed with the heir, so their lineage will continue for generations.

**SHIO OKAWA**
Hmm.

**AMAKUSA**
The Tokugawa government culminated the feudal system, right?

**SHIO OKAWA**
Yes.

**AMAKUSA**
We were aiming to create a nation based on faith that was a bit more free and equal.

**SHIO OKAWA**
There was a class system in the Edo period (1603-1868) as well.

## AMAKUSA

Yes, it was quite fixed.

## SHIO OKAWA

And it consequently led to the Meiji Restoration.

## AMAKUSA

That is right. Many people died in the Meiji Restoration, but there were people who were in a similar circumstance in Kyushu. There were some outstanding people in Kyushu. But they were defeated. Well, China... This happened in the Heian period, too. They had to make the decision of whether to separate from the influence of China's cultural sphere. Even now, the tug of war continues. Christianity still hasn't spread in Japan.

## SHIO OKAWA

Hmm.

# 3

# Japan Must Help the Christian Resistance in Hong Kong

## *Hong Kong is a part of Christian cultural sphere*

### AMAKUSA

But Hong Kong has adopted Western culture as part of Christian culture, so if Christianity is abolished, the Western culture will also disappear. Probably. That is the kind of relationship between them.

Geopolitically, Hong Kong is in a very difficult position. It is located at the edge of China, so if they are surrounded, they have nowhere to run. It is a city with a high-density population, so a large-scale genocide is possible there. If China uses tanks or conducts airstrikes, almost all... a large number of people will die. So, they need to build many boats as soon as possible.

### SHIO OKAWA

As you said, there is not much land there, so there is no place to run.

### AMAKUSA

If they were to run away, they would need to build boats and escape to Taiwan, early on. If the Chinese army came in, they will have to escape to Taiwan, and then escape from Taiwan to another country. China is now trying to create bases around the world, so that there will be no place to escape to. So, there is actually no place the Hong Kong people can run to now. That is why, the most important thing right now is for Japan to stand firm.

## SHIO OKAWA
Yes.

## *Japan should be as willing to take in the Hong Kong people*

## AMAKUSA
If Japan has the willingness to take in the seven million Hong Kong people, they should build a financial center instead of a casino.

## SHIO OKAWA
That is true.

## AMAKUSA
Right? Japan can take in seven million people. Japan is fully capable of that. By doing so, Japan can prosper greatly. It would be like having overseas Chinese come in.

# 4

# The Light of Jesus is Trying to Break Through Marxism by the Power of Faith

## *How Jesus' energy body disperses its light*

**SHIO OKAWA**

Can we assume that you are now reborn as Ms. Agnes Chow?

**AMAKUSA**

Hmm... [*About 5 seconds of silence.*] If I say that, you'll be able to tell my future.

**SHIO OKAWA**

I don't think so. In any era, there are those who die young and those who live to fulfill their mission. They can live a long life, too.

**AMAKUSA**

You can say that we are connected.

**SHIO OKAWA**

Are you two soul siblings?

**AMAKUSA**

Yes. We are on the same level. If you liken Jesus to a fluorescent lamp, Jesus himself is at the central part, and it's surrounded by an array of small lights, like in a chandelier. We are connected like that.

**SHIO OKAWA**

So, is Ms. Agnes Chow "a piece of Jesus"?

**AMAKUSA**

Yeah, a piece.

**SHIO OKAWA**

That is amazing.

**AMAKUSA**

Oscar Wilde and Shiro Amakusa, too. From this, you can see that Shiro Amakusa, Jan Hus, and there are so many others like us.

**SHIO OKAWA**

Ah.

**AMAKUSA**

We are in a similar situation now. And in Japan...

## SHIO OKAWA

So, smaller souls surround the energy body of the great soul called Jesus?

## AMAKUSA

Souls on that level are not composed of one core spirit and five branch spirits*. Instead of "one core, five branch," there are more than 10 additional, smaller branch spirits surrounding the soul group. So, I think we are connected.

## JINMU

Are you soul siblings with Oscar Wilde?

## AMAKUSA

He probably inherited a part of the light of Jesus. I wonder what... Hmm.

## SHIO OKAWA

So, rather than a soul sibling...

## JINMU

You are connected?

---

* In principle, the human soul is composed of six parts, where there is one core spirit and five branch spirits. These are called soul siblings and the six take turns to be born on earth. Furthermore, in the higher dimensions of the Spirit World, the spirits have an enormous amount of energy, so depending on the circumstance, they are able to disperse freely. See the end section of this book.

**SHIO OKAWA**
You branched off of the energy body of the parent soul?

**AMAKUSA**
Hmm. I am like a petal of a sunflower.

**JINMU**
I see.

**AMAKUSA**
I understand that a lot of petals surround the center of a single sunflower. In that sense, I believe we are all connected, but we are not completely equal.

### The light of Jesus will flow in much more from now on

**SHIO OKAWA**
Do you mean that, if we trace back the energy that's flowing into you, we can see that you come from the same source?

**AMAKUSA**
So, I believe that the light of Jesus will be flowing into Agnes Chow.

**SHIO OKAWA**
Do you mean that she will receive more guidance (from Jesus)?

**AMAKUSA**

That is right. And that's why Happy Science is eager to support her, too.

**SHIO OKAWA**

Jesus is truly a hard worker.

**AMAKUSA**

Some while ago, in Taiwan, too, Jesus said to oppose China, but he wants to say that in Hong Kong and also in Canada.

**SHIO OKAWA**

I see.

**AMAKUSA**

Jesus is now passionately advocating opposition to China and trying to break through Marxism with faith.

# 5

# The Wide Range of Roles Christian Civilization Played Throughout Human History

## *The world wanted to entrust Asia to Japan during the Meiji period*

**AMAKUSA**

In the Tokugawa era, Japan lost to what are now the Chinese, but after China (Qing Dynasty) lost to Britain in the Opium Wars, they started to crumble. Japan increased in power, and the governance over South Korea and China was entrusted to Japan by the developed countries. It wasn't that the Japanese army went out of control during WWII. Japan had gained trust after the Sino-Japanese war.

Britain, America, and other nations were all located far away, so they decided to entrust Japan, a closer country, with those countries. Japan was already a member of the developed nations, or "G7" then. Actually, Japan was a member of "G5" at that time. After winning the Sino-Japanese war and Russo-Japanese war, Japan consolidated its position. It was already a part of the G5.

So, it wasn't that Japan suddenly went crazy and out of control during WWII. The global trend was to entrust Asia to Japan. They couldn't trust China, and they couldn't trust North Korea and South Korea (the Korean Peninsula), either.

## *Southern China is prospering because it adopted British culture*

### AMAKUSA

Hong Kong was a colony. India was a big religious nation, so Britain couldn't successfully colonize India; they only exploited it. But Britain was able to lead Hong Kong to prosperity. Even Shanghai was able to enjoy the British prosperity. Southern China is prospering now because of the European, especially the British, culture.

### SHIO OKAWA

I've heard that some British officers who remain in the upper echelon of the Hong Kong police are taking the side of those cracking down on protestors.

### AMAKUSA

The Hong Kong protestors are becoming more furious. They are using firebombs, right? They are becoming more violent, but the authorities are the ones arming themselves with artillery and other weapons. They may possibly come in with armored vehicles soon.

**SHIO OKAWA**

Ms. Shaku (of the Happiness Realization Party) said that the news media are reporting what's contrary to the fact. She said, "The protestors are not armed with artilleries. The police and the army are the ones equipped with and are using them. Yet, the protestors are the ones who are considered dangerous."

**AMAKUSA**

Yes. They are reporting the news like that in mainland China.

**SHIO OKAWA**

I see.

**AMAKUSA**

But the seven million people are now held hostage. If things turn out for the worse, it could lead to a terrible tragedy. So, although President Trump may be preoccupied with other things...

**SHIO OKAWA**

Can President Trump receive guidance from Jesus?

**AMAKUSA**

President Trump's mind is focused on trade issues now.

**SHIO OKAWA**

I see. In regards to China...

**AMAKUSA**

Hmm. He cannot handle the military issue at the same time. The United States is expanding their front line; they must deal with Iran now, in addition to North Korea. He needs an advisor if he wants to make a move.

## *The connection between Jesus' spirit group and Hong Xiuquan, a Christian revolutionary of Qing China*

**SHIO OKAWA**

The guardian spirit of Agnes Chow also mentioned the name, Hong Xiuquan. What kind of connection do you have with him?

**AMAKUSA**

Hmm... I think our higher selves work together.

**SHIO OKAWA**

Ah, I see. I believe Mr. Hong Xiuquan was like a split soul of Zoroaster[*]. And you are also like that (split soul) of Jesus.

---

[*] Zoroaster (Before 8th century BC) was the founder of Zoroastrianism. He preached the duality of good and evil in the regions of ancient Iran. Later, he reincarnated as Mani (215-275) and became the founder of Manichaeism. A ninth-dimensional existence. See *The Laws of the Sun* (New York: IRH Press, 2018).

## AMAKUSA

Hmm. Well... Even if spirits from a high dimension emerge as religious figures in the current era, they would be crushed as "dissidents" by the opposing forces. The modern military is powerful enough to do that.

That's the difficult part. We need to take into account politics if we want to bring about a religious revolution. So, we must not let Japan undermine itself as the left-wing supporters advocate. Actually, if you support Hong Kong, you may appear to be left-wing. But if Japan becomes weak... South Korea is saying that they will seize Japan's islands (Sado Island and Tsushima Island) all the way to Kyushu. So, Japan must become stronger. China is increasing its armament enormously.

Whether Hong Kong will end up being made an example of, or set off in the direction toward a new revolution, will be ultimately decided by El Cantare. The soul of Jesus often loses in this physical world. The soul of El Cantare is the one who wins. I believe your activities have a lot to do with that.

## SHIO OKAWA

They are crucial.

## The surprising past life of Francis Xavier, a Christian who went on a missionary work in Japan

**AMAKUSA**

We started an independence movement in Kyushu, but were annihilated.

**JINMU**

At the time, what was your mission that you were born to fulfill? Did you have a plan to make Japan a Christian nation?

**AMAKUSA**

Well, Paul was already in Japan doing missionary work.

**SHIO OKAWA & JINMU**

Paul?

**JINMU**

Please tell us more about it.

**AMAKUSA**

Sure. He was (Francis) Xavier.

**SHIO OKAWA**

Ah!

**JINMU**
Xavier was actually Paul?

**SHIO OKAWA**
He was the reincarnation of Paul?

**AMAKUSA**
Yes.

**JINMU**
Wow!

**SHIO OKAWA**
I was watching a TV show about Xavier this morning, and learned about how he went to India to spread Christianity. He really went all over the world.

**AMAKUSA**
He went all over the world.

**JINMU**
He is known worldwide.

**AMAKUSA**
It's the same as what you are doing now. He devoted his life to spread the Truth back then, too.

**SHIO OKAWA**
So, he did.

**AMAKUSA**
He even turned *daimyos* (Japanese feudal lords) of Kyushu into Christians.

**JINMU**
That's true.

**AMAKUSA**
It spread quite widely. The top leaders of the nation were powerful.

**SHIO OKAWA**
Even if we assume Confucianism was incorporated, I believe there would have been something lacking.

**AMAKUSA**
Yes. We couldn't win. We knew we couldn't have won.

**SHIO OKAWA**
I meant, from the heavenly world...

**JINMU**
The teachings...

**AMAKUSA**

Oh, it wasn't enough. It was not enough.

**SHIO OKAWA**

When looking at that age from the eyes of God, could you give an example of what you think was lacking?

**AMAKUSA**

Hmm... It lacked love. In other words, the idea of human rights was taken lightly.

**JINMU**

I see.

**SHIO OKAWA**

The Tokugawa family created a system where they could continue their family line for generations (by implementing Confucianism).

**AMAKUSA**

Yes, yes. Confucianism helps to create a society based on class.

**SHIO OKAWA**

That's true.

**JINMU**

It is a system that prevents rebellions.

**AMAKUSA**

The modern democratic system allows individuals to develop their skills.

## *Jesus' soul engages in a wide range of activities*

**SHIO OKAWA**

It really does connect to "Power to the People." (Song released by John Lennon in 1971.)

**AMAKUSA**

That's right. We are the same. I can sing John Lennon's song, too.

**SHIO OKAWA**

You can. I see.

**AMAKUSA**

Jesus' soul is now dispersed across a wide range of fields. He is appearing in quite a lot of places.

**SHIO OKAWA**

So, the hidden side of Jesus is...

**AMAKUSA**

Yes. Perhaps not the "golden dust," but more like "golden bullions" are spread everywhere.

**SHIO OKAWA**

I see...

**JINMU**

So, are there people like that in all kinds of fields?

**AMAKUSA**

You know, El Cantare is watching from a higher level. Usually, Jesus is the one who sacrifices his life.

**SHIO OKAWA**

But that's his role, right?

**AMAKUSA**

Yes. Most of the time, Jesus and Zoroaster are born to be martyred.

**SHIO OKAWA**

So, you really are Metatron[*].

---

[*] According to UFO readings conducted by Happy Science, an alien named Metatron from Planet Include in Sagittarius is a part of the space soul of Jesus Christ (Amor), and was born 6,500 years ago in Mesopotamia.

# 6

# The Wave Created by Heaven to Bring About the Downfall of China, a Nation With the Population of 1.4 Billion

## *I shouldn't say where the revolutionary leaders are in China*

**JINMU**

By the way, do you know where Hong Xiuquan is now?

**AMAKUSA**

Hmm. What do you mean by "where"? How should I put it?

**JINMU**

I mean in this world...

**AMAKUSA**

Do you need the exact address?

**JINMU**

[*Laughs.*] (In the spiritual interview with Hong Xiuquan) He sounded like he lives in China now.

## AMAKUSA

Ah! That may be true.

## SHIO OKAWA

Does that mean that there is a secret weapon that we don't know of?

## AMAKUSA

That is... Even if Hong Kong gets suppressed, other rebelling forces will emerge from within (China) such as Uyghur, Tibet and Inner Mongolia. But I can't say who they are. They will be crushed.

## JINMU

I see.

## SHIO OKAWA

They were sent to lay the groundwork to bring down the Chinese regime...

## AMAKUSA

It is impossible for a person to do this, so many people are sent into different locations through various ways. The heavenly powers are working to bring about the downfall of China, a big nation with the population of 1.4 billion.

As a consequence, the power of Ahriman[*] is growing stronger, too.

**SHIO OKAWA**
I see.

**JINMU**
So, in that case, there are other secret weapons besides Hong Xiuquan...

**AMAKUSA**
Yes. Of course, yes.

**JINMU**
I see.

**AMAKUSA**
Of course, there are.

**JINMU**
So, these people are like the branch spirits of the ninth-dimensional grand spirits...

---

[*] The God of Darkness that appears in Zoroastrianism. He is the polar opposite of the God of Goodness, Ahura Mazda. Additionally, it was revealed that he is a devilish being from outer space that is worshipped by malicious extraterrestrials.

**AMAKUSA**

Well, I cannot reveal that much yet. No one should be able to tell who they are until they appear as leaders.

**SHIO OKAWA**

El Cantare, Himself, is taking action on earth. So, those who are working toward that direction need to be born here in this world and take action to change the world.

**AMAKUSA**

In short, we are trying to westernize China now.

## The wave of modernization in China and India

**SHIO OKAWA**

Does this mean that spirits in the heavenly world mainly believe that westernization would protect human rights and that each individual will be able to blossom a bit more?

**AMAKUSA**

It is quite harsh to be born as a farmer and to die as a farmer in China today. India will also need to go through a religious reform soon. There's a little bit of time lag there. There are many gods there, but the time will come when their religion gets organized on a higher level. At that time, someone should appear in India.

Modernization of China and India, countries with a large population, is a tremendously important task now. So many leaders are sent in, although some become sacrifices.

## He was hampered by the Tokugawa government and seclusion policy

**SHIO OKAWA**
Did you reincarnate after you were born as Shiro Amakusa?

**AMAKUSA**
Well, uh... Hmm.

**SHIO OKAWA**
Oh! Are you Ms. Agnes Chow?

**AMAKUSA**
Hmm.

**SHIO OKAWA**
Does it mean yes?

**AMAKUSA**
As I said, I am a petal.

**SHIO OKAWA**
I see. I see. You mean that you are part of the energy body connected to Jesus?

## AMAKUSA

Yes. So, as such, I am planning to work a miracle. Well, Jesus also... You may disagree, but Jesus himself was executed as an individual, and his activities did not reach the level of Shiro Amakusa's rebellion. If I may say so. I may be better than you think. The only problem was that it did not spread much afterwards. The government was powerful. The Tokugawa government which lasted three hundred years was much stronger. Yes. And they used a new tactic called "national seclusion." They only traded with the Netherlands at Dejima in Nagasaki.

## SHIO OKAWA

I see.

## AMAKUSA

Well, through this, Japan was able to create their unique culture. And China declined after the Ming dynasty. After the Ming and Qing dynasties, China declined. So in a sense, the good old culture of China was preserved in the Tokugawa period of Japan.

## SHIO OKAWA

Hmm.

## The power relationships of modern Chinese religion in the Spirit World

### JINMU

I am curious about the current situation of the Chinese gods. For example, Confucius...

### AMAKUSA

No, Confucius is no longer there.

### SHIO OKAWA

He is not there.

### AMAKUSA

No. He has other work to do.

### SHIO OKAWA

Where is he? Is he in outer space?

### JINMU

Other work? Is it related to outer space?

### AMAKUSA

He has absolutely no interest in the governance of China.

### JINMU

Absolutely none?

**AMAKUSA**

No, he can't. It is over. It is over.

**SHIO OKAWA**

But yesterday, Ms. Agnes Chow stated that Lao Tzu is helping Hong Kong a bit. (See Chapter 2.)

**AMAKUSA**

It's a Jiangshi-like (Zombie-like) movement.

**SHIO OKAWA**

Oh, but materialism...

**AMAKUSA**

People still have such folk beliefs.

**SHIO OKAWA**

So, they want to bring together those kinds of people?

**AMAKUSA**

They practice sorcery and hold funerals, and you can find such psychics in China. People still have folk beliefs. They still maintain the traditions of sorcery and wizardry. Under the communist rule, these things are hidden behind, but they still practice them.

## SHIO OKAWA

That's true. Then, what do you think should be done about the heavenly world of China?

## JINMU

For example, how about those known as great emperors, such as Emperor Taizong of Tang? Do they come in to support you?

## AMAKUSA

I am Shiro Amakusa, you know?

## JINMU

I'm sorry. [*Laughs.*]

## AMAKUSA

Who do you think you are asking?

## JINMU

Sorry, I was just curious about what is happening in the Spirit World of China.

## AMAKUSA

Hmm. Well, China is presenting one way of looking at the world. Like the Roman Empire, China presented its worldview, where an emperor appears and builds a dynasty every few hundred years.

In the current democratic system, people have become impatient and the change of "dynasty" happens within a shorter span.

## SHIO OKAWA

But if they are willing to unify a dynasty at the cost of the citizens, Hell will expand every time people are born there.

## AMAKUSA

They will shed a lot of blood. Ahh. You, Mr. Liu Bei, could not stay in China. So, you "transformed into a panda" and lived there. (Note: In a past spiritual investigation, it was revealed that Shio Okawa was Liu Bei in a past life.)

## SHIO OKAWA

Oh, I've managed to stay alive somehow.

## AMAKUSA

You must be hiding among a herd of 1,800 (pandas) and taking command of them. You are protecting the Sichuan province.

## SHIO OKAWA

I want to revive China once again in some way.

## AMAKUSA

Even Guan Yu has become a god for the present, but he

hasn't reached the level where he can lead a whole nation. Among the great figures of the past, some went to China. But it's a bit difficult to view the entire China of today.

## SHIO OKAWA

Does the Xi Jinping side hold all the power?

## AMAKUSA

He is extremely strong. His demonic power is extremely strong. Actually, I think he always appears as the enemy of the people.

# 7

# Aiming for a System Where Your Life is Not Determined by Your Birth

## *A new Meiji Restoration movement is necessary*

**SHIO OKAWA**

So basically, that's how the idea that democracy is important and that we must spread democracy based on faith comes forth.

**AMAKUSA**

Democracy means that your life is not necessarily determined by your birth, right?

**SHIO OKAWA**

Especially, when we are born as a commoner, we deeply understand this value of democracy.

**AMAKUSA**

If that's the case, the same thing must happen in India. They have a caste system there, so it needs to be broken down. They need to bring about a Meiji Restoration-like revolution. So, they need a revolutionary like Ryoma Sakamoto.

## *The reformation of Japan will occur once again and will spread to all of Asia*

### SHIO OKAWA

Like the way Ryoma Sakamoto ultimately succeeded in his restoration of imperial rule, we must work hard in restoring an ideal governance.

### AMAKUSA

The result will come out in Japan soon.

### SHIO OKAWA

I see.

### AMAKUSA

Yes. Japan will go through reformation once again. The Happiness Realization Party doesn't have much power now, but it will gain more power in the future. So, I believe that the reformation of the regime will occur. This is something we can look forward to in the 21$^{st}$ century. Japan, China, North Korea and India will all change.

### SHIO OKAWA

I see.

### AMAKUSA

Yes.

**SHIO OKAWA**

Is that part of Heaven's plan?

**AMAKUSA**

Yes. Many revolutionaries like myself have already been born. They will do it, without a doubt.

**SHIO OKAWA**

I see.

## Numerous revolutionaries are born in Christian and Islamic countries

**AMAKUSA**

In the spiritual interview with the guardian spirit of Agnes Chow, she mentioned that we may have a connection. And I say we do. You can assume that a piece of Jesus' soul is inside...

**SHIO OKAWA**

Does that mean his light dwells within you?

**AMAKUSA**

Yes, that's correct. Well, I am not exactly his "replacement." It's not like that. But there are numerous souls in the modern era that have descended from the light of Jesus. In the current era, there are so many of them now.

Jesus is working hard. There are 2.2 billion Christians after all. Islam is also spreading now. Although the Japanese people don't know about it, there are many great souls who have been born among Muslims. Currently, great souls have been mainly born among Christians and Muslims. Hm.

## What if Nagasaki were known as a land of Christians?

**JINMU**
Shimabara is located in Nagasaki, but Nagasaki is also the land where the atomic bomb was dropped. At that time, were you watching it happen from Heaven?

**AMAKUSA**
Well, suffering. It is a land of suffering.

**JINMU**
Hmm.

**AMAKUSA**
They (Americans) wouldn't have been able to drop it, if they thought it was a land of Christians. But they lacked knowledge, or they did not know about it. They probably only had their eyes on the shipyard. Hmm.

## God wishes to spread Hong Kong's prosperity to China

### SHIO OKAWA

Do you have any messages for the people of Hong Kong? At the beginning, you said that their songs are reaching Heaven. What king of thoughts or feelings should the Hong Kong people hold onto to receive more light from Heaven?

### AMAKUSA

Like Master Okawa stated in his lecture* a few years ago, you should say with confidence that it is God's wish that Hong Kong's prosperity spreads to China in the future, and not move in the direction for Hong Kong and Taiwan to fall under the control of China.

It's not good enough that Hong Kong gains the right of self-government. We need to change China itself. China lacks the next national policy. They don't know what to do. That is why they are trying to invade other countries with force, as if they are implementing colonialism during medieval times. That's what they are trying to do.

---

* See the aforementioned *Love for the Future*, Chapter 2 "The Fact and the Truth."

**SHIO OKAWA**

What they are doing right now is putting in action what they learned in world history, like what empires of the past did...

**AMAKUSA**

So, it would be desirable that Hong Kong's prosperity spreads.

**SHIO OKAWA**

Hong Kong's prosperity will allow more people to exercise their individual abilities and...

**AMAKUSA**

Actually, Xi Jinping thinks it is impossible to govern an unstable nation where rulers may change each time an election is held. He sees Japanese election like that. But this way of thinking is exactly what was held by those in power during the Tokugawa era. That's how outdated his level of recognition is. This must be changed.

**SHIO OKAWA**

I see.

**AMAKUSA**

We are supporting you, too. The success in this world is not everything, but this will have impact on the world.

God does not wish for today's China to take control of this world.

## The situation of the surveillance state of China

### SHIO OKAWA
Sorry, we're running out of time, but I would like to ask one last question. We've heard what the people who actually went to China said. Before they went there, they heard that China is a surveillance state, that human rights are extremely restricted, and that they don't have faith. But when they actually went there, they didn't feel that way and thought that people were living normal lives.

### AMAKUSA
Regular tourists would probably feel that way.

### SHIO OKAWA
Yes. But if you actually live there...

### AMAKUSA
People who are already living there are under constant surveillance. The situation is the same as the Tokugawa era. Organizations like "Gonin-gumi" (The five household groups that held collective responsibility for crime and watched over one another) are monitoring one another and acting as whistleblowers.

**SHIO OKAWA**
It is like the situation in North Korea.

**AMAKUSA**
It is the same.

**SHIO OKAWA**
I see.

**AMAKUSA**
We need to put an end to this way of thinking.

**SHIO OKAWA**
I understand.

**INTERVIEWERS**
Thank you very much.

**AMAKUSA**
Sure.

# Chapter Four

# Spiritual Messages
from Hannah Arendt

Recorded September 4, 2019
Special Lecture Hall, Happy Science,
Japan

# Hannah Arendt (1906 - 1975)

A political scientist and philosopher. She was born into a German-Jewish family. At the age of 18, she entered the University of Marburg and studied under Martin Heidegger. Later, she attended the University of Freiburg and studied under Edmund Husserl. Afterward, she went on to the University of Heidelberg and studied under Karl Jaspers. In 1928, while studying under Husserl, she wrote her dissertation on the concept of love in the thought of Saint Augustine, and received a doctoral degree in philosophy at Heidelberg. After the Nazi assumption of power in 1933, she fled to Paris and engaged in supporting Jewish refugees there. In 1951, she released one of her main works, *The Origins of Totalitarianism*, which traced the roots of Nazism and Stalinism by focusing on both anti-Semitism and imperialism. Among her other major works are: *The Human Condition*, *On Revolution* and *Eichmann in Jerusalem: A Report on the Banality of Evil*.

## Interviewers from Happy Science[*]:

### Shio Okawa
Aide to Master

### Sakurako Jinmu
Managing Director
Chief Secretary of First Secretarial Division
Religious Affairs Headquarters

*The opinions of the spirit do not necessarily reflect those of Happy Science Group.*
*For the mechanism behind spiritual messages, see end section.*

---

[*] Interviewers are listed in the order that they appear in the transcript.
Their professional titles represent their positions at the time of the interview.

## *"I am guiding Agnes Chow"*

**RYUHO OKAWA**
Ms. Hannah Arendt, Ms. Hannah Arendt.

**HANNAH ARENDT**
This is Hannah Arendt.

**SHIO OKAWA**
Thank you for coming again.

**ARENDT**
Yes, sure.

**SHIO OKAWA**
Currently, Ms. Agnes Chow is taking action in Hong Kong, and we've heard that she is receiving guidance from you.

**ARENDT**
Yes, yes.

**SHIO OKAWA**
Is that correct?

**ARENDT**
Yes, that's right. I am guiding (Agnes Chow).

**SHIO OKAWA**

Do you have a spiritual connection to Ms. Agnes Chow?

**ARENDT**

Hmm... [*About 5 seconds of silence.*] It seems that something similar to the persecution of the Jewish by the Nazis may happen again. I spent my whole life fighting totalitarianism and fascism...

**SHIO OKAWA**

Yes. That's exactly...

**ARENDT**

Uh huh. That's exactly what will happen. So, it is important to inform a great number of people about this, not after it happens, but before it happens.

**SHIO OKAWA**

We must inform them?

**ARENDT**

Master Ryuho Okawa has been studying about it. It is usually very difficult for religious groups to talk about things like this, but you can now.

**SHIO OKAWA**

Yes.

**ARENDT**

So, it has to do with me, and it also has to do with Master Ryuho Okawa. Now, I am ideologically...

**SHIO OKAWA**

Fighting?

**ARENDT**

It is one of the subjects I am researching now, even after I returned to Heaven.

**SHIO OKAWA**

I see.

**ARENDT**

Yes, so I am supporting her. As a soul, we've met numerous times in relation to Christianity and Judaism, so she is one of my friends.*

---

* See *On Happiness Revolution: A Spiritual Interview with Hannah Arendt* (Tokyo: HS Press, 2014).

## SHIO OKAWA

She is your friend.

## ARENDT

Yes.

## SAKURAKO JINMU

Is your soul related to hers?

## ARENDT

Hmm. Not exactly, but we are friends.

## *We must not repeat the tragedy in history caused by totalitarianism*

## SHIO OKAWA

From your perspective, a totalitarian country is once again about to emerge.

## ARENDT

Yes. While I was alive, I couldn't analyze fascism in China after the Mao Zedong revolution. I passed away in 1975, and Mao Zedong passed away in 1976. Because we lived in the same era, I couldn't analyze it fully. But now, Master Ryuho Okawa is doing that, so I should offer my support.

**SHIO OKAWA**

So, as for your opinion...

**ARENDT**

I think that we must not repeat that tragedy.

**SHIO OKAWA**

I see. I understand.

**JINMU**

Thank you very much.

**ARENDT**

Sure.

**SHIO OKAWA**

We appreciate your guidance and support.

**ARENDT**

Sure.

# Afterword

This book is valuable; you can deeply understand the true meaning behind the confrontation between Mr. Xi Jinping, who aims to put the Earth under the control of darkness, and Ms. Agnes Chow, who carries in her a piece of the soul of Jesus Christ.

The Hong Kong Revolution is indeed God's Revolution.

God is trying to create a world of freedom, democracy and faith.

And Hong Kong passionately shows that "Now is the time to fight for freedom."

It is not against the current Constitution of Japan to mobilize the Self-Defense Forces and send it off the shores of Hong Kong under the pretext of protecting 20,000 Japanese residents. It will certainly be an indication of Japan's stance against the next possible Taiwan crisis.

Japan must now send out the correct signal toward the world.

*Ryuho Okawa*
*Master & CEO of Happy Science Group*
*Founder and President of the Happiness Realization Party*
*September 5, 2019*

# ABOUT THE AUTHOR

Founder and CEO of Happy Science Group.

Ryuho Okawa was born on July 7th 1956, in Tokushima, Japan. After graduating from the University of Tokyo with a law degree, he joined a Tokyo-based trading house. While working at its New York headquarters, he studied international finance at the Graduate Center of the City University of New York. In 1981, he attained Great Enlightenment and became aware that he is El Cantare with a mission to bring salvation to all humankind.

In 1986, he established Happy Science. It now has members in over 165 countries across the world, with more than 700 branches and temples as well as 10,000 missionary houses around the world.

He has given over 3,400 lectures (of which more than 150 are in English) and published over 3,000 books (of which more than 600 are Spiritual Interview Series), and many are translated into 40 languages. Along with *The Laws of the Sun* and *The Laws Of Messiah*, many of the books have become best sellers or million sellers. To date, Happy Science has produced 25 movies. The original story and original concept were given by the Executive Producer Ryuho Okawa. He has also composed music and written lyrics of over 450 pieces.

Moreover, he is the Founder of Happy Science University and Happy Science Academy (Junior and Senior High School), Founder and President of the Happiness Realization Party, Founder and Honorary Headmaster of Happy Science Institute of Government and Management, Founder of IRH Press Co., Ltd., and the Chairperson of NEW STAR PRODUCTION Co., Ltd. and ARI Production Co., Ltd.

# WHAT IS EL CANTARE?

El Cantare means "the Light of the Earth," and is the Supreme God of the Earth who has been guiding humankind since the beginning of Genesis. He is whom Jesus called Father and Muhammad called Allah, and is *Ame-no-Mioya-Gami*, Japanese Father God. Different parts of El Cantare's core consciousness have descended to Earth in the past, once as Alpha and another as Elohim. His branch spirits, such as Shakyamuni Buddha and Hermes, have descended to Earth many times and helped to flourish many civilizations. To unite various religions and to integrate various fields of study in order to build a new civilization on Earth, a part of the core consciousness has descended to Earth as Master Ryuho Okawa.

**Alpha** is a part of the core consciousness of El Cantare who descended to Earth around 330 million years ago. Alpha preached Earth's Truths to harmonize and unify Earth-born humans and space people who came from other planets.

**Elohim** is a part of El Cantare's core consciousness who descended to Earth around 150 million years ago. He gave wisdom, mainly on the differences of light and darkness, good and evil.

**Ame-no-Mioya-Gami (Japanese Father God)** is the Creator God and the Father God who appears in the ancient literature, *Hotsuma Tsutae*. It is believed that He descended on the foothills of Mt. Fuji about 30,000 years ago and built the Fuji dynasty, which is the root of the Japanese civilization. With justice as the central pillar, Ame-no-Mioya-Gami's teachings spread to ancient civilizations of other countries in the world.

**Shakyamuni Buddha** was born as a prince into the Shakya Clan in India around 2,600 years ago. When he was 29 years old, he renounced the world and sought enlightenment. He later attained Great Enlightenment and founded Buddhism.

**Hermes** is one of the 12 Olympian gods in Greek mythology, but the spiritual Truth is that he taught the teachings of love and progress around 4,300 years ago that became the origin of the current Western civilization. He is a hero that truly existed.

**Ophealis** was born in Greece around 6,500 years ago and was the leader who took an expedition to as far as Egypt. He is the God of miracles, prosperity, and arts, and is known as Osiris in the Egyptian mythology.

**Rient Arl Croud** was born as a king of the ancient Incan Empire around 7,000 years ago and taught about the mysteries of the mind. In the heavenly world, he is responsible for the interactions that take place between various planets.

**Thoth** was an almighty leader who built the golden age of the Atlantic civilization around 12,000 years ago. In the Egyptian mythology, he is known as god Thoth.

**Ra Mu** was a leader who built the golden age of the civilization of Mu around 17,000 years ago. As a religious leader and a politician, he ruled by uniting religion and politics.

# WHAT IS A SPIRITUAL MESSAGE?

We are all spiritual beings living on this earth. The following is the mechanism behind Master Ryuho Okawa's spiritual messages.

## 1 You are a spirit

People are born into this world to gain wisdom through various experiences and return to the other world when their lives end. We are all spirits and repeat this cycle in order to refine our souls.

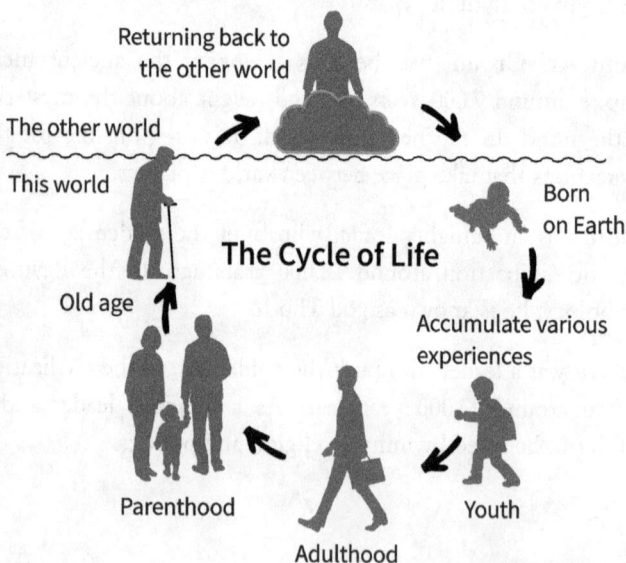

Returning back to the other world

The other world

This world

The Cycle of Life

Born on Earth

Old age

Accumulate various experiences

Parenthood

Adulthood

Youth

## 2  You have a guardian spirit

Guardian spirits are those who protect the people who are living on this earth. Each of us has a guardian spirit that watches over us and guides us from the other world. They were us in our past life, and are identical in how we think.

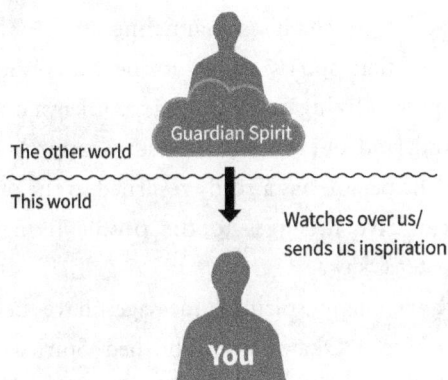

## 3  How spiritual messages work

Master Ryuho Okawa, through his enlightenment, is capable of summoning any spirit from anywhere in the world, including the spirit world.

Master Okawa's way of receiving spiritual messages is fundamentally different from that of other psychic mediums who undergo trances and are thereby completely taken over by the spirits they are channeling.

Master Okawa's attainment of a high level of enlightenment enables him to retain full control of his consciousness and body throughout the duration of the spiritual message. To allow the spirits to express their own thoughts and personalities freely, however, Master Okawa usually softens the dominancy of his consciousness. This way, he is able to keep his own philosophies out of the way and ensure that the spiritual messages are pure expressions of the spirits he is channeling.

Since guardian spirits think at the same subconscious level as the person living on earth, Master Okawa can summon the spirit and find out what the person on earth is actually thinking. If the person has already returned to the other world, the spirit can give messages to the people living on earth through Master Okawa.

Since 2009, many spiritual messages have been openly recorded by Master Okawa and published. Spiritual messages from the guardian spirits of people living today such as Donald Trump, former Japanese Prime Minister Shinzo Abe and Chinese President Xi Jinping, as well as spiritual messages sent from the spirit world by Jesus Christ, Muhammad, Thomas Edison, Mother Teresa, Steve Jobs and Nelson Mandela are just a tiny pack of spiritual messages that were published so far.

Domestically, in Japan, these spiritual messages are being read by a wide range of politicians and mass media, and the high-level contents of these books are delivering an impact even more on politics, news and public opinion. In recent years, there have been spiritual messages recorded in English, and

English translations are being done on the spiritual messages given in Japanese. These have been published overseas, one after another, and have started to shake the world.

**①** The guardian spirit /
spirit in the other world...

**②** Goes inside Master Okawa
in this world

**③** Master Okawa speaks
the words of the guardian spirit /
spirit

*For more about spiritual messages and a complete list of books in the Spiritual Interview Series, visit okawabooks.com*

# ABOUT HAPPY SCIENCE

Happy Science is a global movement that empowers individuals to find purpose and spiritual happiness and to share that happiness with their families, societies, and the world. With more than 12 million members around the world, Happy Science aims to increase awareness of spiritual truths and expand our capacity for love, compassion, and joy so that together we can create the kind of world we all wish to live in.

Activities at Happy Science are based on the Principle of Happiness (Love, Wisdom, Self-Reflection, and Progress). This principle embraces worldwide philosophies and beliefs, transcending boundaries of culture and religions.

**Love** teaches us to give ourselves freely without expecting anything in return; it encompasses giving, nurturing, and forgiving.

**Wisdom** leads us to the insights of spiritual truths, and opens us to the true meaning of life and the will of God (the universe, the highest power, Buddha).

**Self-Reflection** brings a mindful, nonjudgmental lens to our thoughts and actions to help us find our truest selves—the essence of our souls—and deepen our connection to the highest power. It helps us attain a clean and peaceful mind and leads us to the right life path.

**Progress** emphasizes the positive, dynamic aspects of our spiritual growth—actions we can take to manifest and spread happiness around the world. It's a path that not only expands our soul growth, but also furthers the collective potential of the world we live in.

## PROGRAMS AND EVENTS

The doors of Happy Science are open to all. We offer a variety of programs and events, including self-exploration and self-growth programs, spiritual seminars, meditation and contemplation sessions, study groups, and book events.

Our programs are designed to:
* Deepen your understanding of your purpose and meaning in life
* Improve your relationships and increase your capacity to love unconditionally
* Attain peace of mind, decrease anxiety and stress, and feel positive
* Gain deeper insights and a broader perspective on the world
* Learn how to overcome life's challenges
  ... and much more.

*For more information, visit happy-science.org.*

## OUR ACTIVITIES

Happy Science does other various activities to provide support for those in need.

♦ **You Are An Angel! General Incorporated Association**

Happy Science has a volunteer network in Japan that encourages and supports children with disabilities as well as their parents and guardians.

♦ **Never Mind School for Truancy**

At 'Never Mind,' we support students who find it very challenging to attend schools in Japan. We also nurture their self-help spirit and power to rebound against obstacles in life based on Master Okawa's teachings and faith.

♦ **"Prevention Against Suicide" Campaign since 2003**

A nationwide campaign to reduce suicides; over 20,000 people commit suicide every year in Japan. "The Suicide Prevention Website-Words of Truth for You-" presents spiritual prescriptions for worries such as depression, lost love, extramarital affairs, bullying and work-related problems, thereby saving many lives.

♦ **Support for Anti-bullying Campaigns**

Happy Science provides support for a group of parents and guardians, Network to Protect Children from Bullying, a general incorporated foundation launched in Japan to end bullying, including those that can even be called a criminal offense. So far, the network received more than 5,000 cases and resolved 90% of them.

- **The Golden Age Scholarship**

  This scholarship is granted to students who can contribute greatly and bring a hopeful future to the world.

- **Success No.1**
  **Buddha's Truth Afterschool Academy**

  Happy Science has over 180 classrooms throughout Japan and in several cities around the world that focus on afterschool education for children. The education focuses on faith and morals in addition to supporting children's school studies.

- **Angel Plan V**

  For children under the age of kindergarten, Happy Science holds classes for nurturing healthy, positive, and creative boys and girls.

- **Future Stars Training Department**

  The Future Stars Training Department was founded within the Happy Science Media Division with the goal of nurturing talented individuals to become successful in the performing arts and entertainment industry.

- **NEW STAR PRODUCTION Co., Ltd.**
  **ARI Production Co., Ltd.**

  We have companies to nurture actors and actresses, artists, and vocalists. They are also involved in film production.

# CONTACT INFORMATION

Happy Science is a worldwide organization with branches and temples around the globe. For a comprehensive list, visit the worldwide directory at *happy-science.org*. The following are some of the many Happy Science locations:

## UNITED STATES AND CANADA

### New York
79 Franklin St., New York, NY 10013, USA
Phone: 1-212-343-7972
Fax: 1-212-343-7973
Email: ny@happy-science.org
Website: happyscience-usa.org

### New Jersey
66 Hudson St., #2R, Hoboken, NJ 07030, USA
Phone: 1-201-313-0127
Email: nj@happy-science.org
Website: happyscience-usa.org

### Chicago
2300 Barrington Rd., Suite #400,
Hoffman Estates, IL 60169, USA
Phone: 1-630-937-3077
Email: chicago@happy-science.org
Website: happyscience-usa.org

### Florida
5208 8th St., Zephyrhills, FL 33542, USA
Phone: 1-813-715-0000
Fax: 1-813-715-0010
Email: florida@happy-science.org
Website: happyscience-usa.org

### Atlanta
1874 Piedmont Ave., NE Suite 360-C
Atlanta, GA 30324, USA
Phone: 1-404-892-7770
Email: atlanta@happy-science.org
Website: happyscience-usa.org

### San Francisco
525 Clinton St.
Redwood City, CA 94062, USA
Phone & Fax: 1-650-363-2777
Email: sf@happy-science.org
Website: happyscience-usa.org

### Los Angeles
1590 E. Del Mar Blvd., Pasadena, CA 91106, USA
Phone: 1-626-395-7775
Fax: 1-626-395-7776
Email: la@happy-science.org
Website: happyscience-usa.org

### Orange County
16541 Gothard St. Suite 104
Huntington Beach, CA 92647
Phone: 1-714-659-1501
Email: oc@happy-science.org
Website: happyscience-usa.org

### San Diego
7841 Balboa Ave. Suite #202
San Diego, CA 92111, USA
Phone: 1-626-395-7775
Fax: 1-626-395-7776
E-mail: sandiego@happy-science.org
Website: happyscience-usa.org

### Hawaii
Phone: 1-808-591-9772
Fax: 1-808-591-9776
Email: hi@happy-science.org
Website: happyscience-usa.org

### Kauai
3343 Kanakolu Street, Suite 5
Lihue, HI 96766, USA
Phone: 1-808-822-7007
Fax: 1-808-822-6007
Email: kauai-hi@happy-science.org
Website: happyscience-usa.org

## Toronto
845 The Queensway
Etobicoke, ON M8Z 1N6, Canada
Phone: 1-416-901-3747
Email: toronto@happy-science.org
Website: happy-science.ca

## Vancouver
#201-2607 East 49th Avenue,
Vancouver, BC, V5S 1J9, Canada
Phone: 1-604-437-7735
Fax: 1-604-437-7764
Email: vancouver@happy-science.org
Website: happy-science.ca

## INTERNATIONAL

## Tokyo
1-6-7 Togoshi, Shinagawa,
Tokyo, 142-0041, Japan
Phone: 81-3-6384-5770
Fax: 81-3-6384-5776
Email: tokyo@happy-science.org
Website: happy-science.org

## Seoul
74, Sadang-ro 27-gil,
Dongjak-gu, Seoul, Korea
Phone: 82-2-3478-8777
Fax: 82-2-3478-9777
Email: korea@happy-science.org
Website: happyscience-korea.org

## London
3 Margaret St.
London, W1W 8RE United Kingdom
Phone: 44-20-7323-9255
Fax: 44-20-7323-9344
Email: eu@happy-science.org
Website: www.happyscience-uk.org

## Taipei
No. 89, Lane 155, Dunhua N. Road,
Songshan District, Taipei City 105, Taiwan
Phone: 886-2-2719-9377
Fax: 886-2-2719-5570
Email: taiwan@happy-science.org
Website: happyscience-tw.org

## Sydney
516 Pacific Highway, Lane Cove North,
2066 NSW, Australia
Phone: 61-2-9411-2877
Fax: 61-2-9411-2822
Email: sydney@happy-science.org

## Kuala Lumpur
No 22A, Block 2, Jalil Link Jalan Jalil
Jaya 2, Bukit Jalil 57000,
Kuala Lumpur, Malaysia
Phone: 60-3-8998-7877
Fax: 60-3-8998-7977
Email: malaysia@happy-science.org
Website: happyscience.org.my

## Sao Paulo
Rua. Domingos de Morais 1154,
Vila Mariana, Sao Paulo SP
CEP 04010-100, Brazil
Phone: 55-11-5088-3800
Email: sp@happy-science.org
Website: happyscience.com.br

## Kathmandu
Kathmandu Metropolitan City,
Ward No. 15, Ring Road, Kimdol,
Sitapaila Kathmandu, Nepal
Phone: 977-1-427-2931
Email: nepal@happy-science.org

## Jundiai
Rua Congo, 447, Jd. Bonfiglioli
Jundiai-CEP, 13207-340, Brazil
Phone: 55-11-4587-5952
Email: jundiai@happy-science.org

## Kampala
Plot 877 Rubaga Road, Kampala
P.O. Box 34130 Kampala, UGANDA
Phone: 256-79-4682-121
Email: uganda@happy-science.org

# ABOUT HS PRESS

HS Press is an imprint of IRH Press Co., Ltd. IRH Press Co., Ltd., based in Tokyo, was founded in 1987 as a publishing division of Happy Science. IRH Press publishes religious and spiritual books, journals, magazines and also operates broadcast and film production enterprises. For more information, visit *okawabooks.com*.

*Follow us on:*

**f** Facebook: Okawa Books    Instagram: OkawaBooks
 Youtube: Okawa Books    Twitter: Okawa Books
 Pinterest: Okawa Books    Goodreads: Ryuho Okawa

——— **NEWSLETTER** ———

To receive book related news, promotions and events, please subscribe to our newsletter below.

 eepurl.com/bsMeJj

——— **AUDIO / VISUAL MEDIA** ———

**YOUTUBE**          **PODCAST**

Introduction of Ryuho Okawa's titles; topics ranging from self-help, current affairs, spirituality, religion, and the universe.

# BOOKS BY RYUHO OKAWA

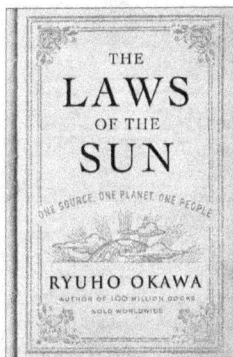

## THE LAWS OF THE SUN

### ONE SOURCE, ONE PLANET, ONE PEOPLE

Paperback • 288 pages • $15.95
ISBN: 978-1-942125-43-3

Imagine if you could ask God why he created this world and what spiritual laws he used to shape us—and everything around us. In The Laws of the Sun, Ryuho Okawa outlines these laws of the universe and provides a road map for living one's life with greater purpose and meaning. This powerful book shows the way to realize true happiness—a happiness that continues from this world through the other.

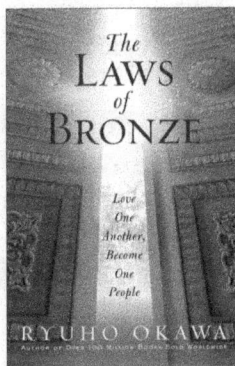

## THE LAWS OF BRONZE

### LOVE ONE ANOTHER, BECOME ONE PEOPLE

Paperback • 224 pages • $15.95
ISBN: 978-1-942125-50-1

This is the 25th volume of the Laws of Series by Ryuho Okawa. Following the releases of The Laws of Mission in 2017 and The Laws of Faith in 2018, this latest volume will help the readers deepen their faith and elevate their awareness to a global scale and even to the cosmic level. This miraculous and inspiring book will show the keys to living a spiritual life of truth regardless of their age, gender, or race.

---

*For a complete list of books, visit okawabooks.com*

## THE LAWS OF JUSTICE

### HOW WE CAN SOLVE WORLD CONFLICTS AND BRING PEACE

Paperback • 208 pages • $15.95
ISBN: 978-1-942125-05-1

This book shows what global justice is from a comprehensive perspective of the Supreme God. Becoming aware of this view will let us embrace differences in beliefs, recognize other peoples divine nature, and love and forgive one another. It will also become the key to solving the issues we face, whether they are religious, political, societal, economic, or academic, and help the world become a better and safer world for all of us living today.

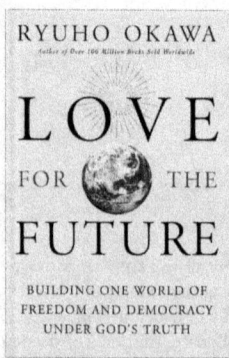

## LOVE FOR THE FUTURE

### BUILDING ONE WORLD OF FREEDOM AND DEMOCRACY UNDER GOD'S TRUTH

Paperback • 312 pages • $15.95
ISBN: 978-1-942125-60-0

This is a compilation of select international lectures given by Ryuho Okawa during his (ongoing) global missionary tours. While conflicting values of justice exists, this book espouses that freedom and democracy are vital principles for global unification that will resolutely foster peace and shared prosperity, if adopted universally.

*For a complete list of books, visit okawabooks.com*

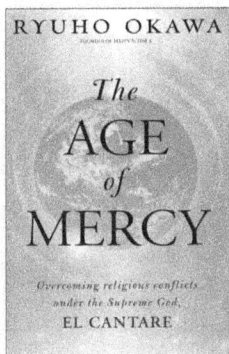

## THE AGE OF MERCY

### OVERCOMING RELIGIOUS CONFLICTS UNDER THE SUPREME GOD, EL CANTARE

Hardcover • 110 pages • $22.95
ISBN: 978-1-943869-51-0

Christians, Muslims, and God-believers
Materialists, communists, and non-believers...

Why do they fight?
When will they say, "it's all right"?
We bring you the messages of salvation from the Primordial God,
Who has been nurturing us humans since the beginning of time.

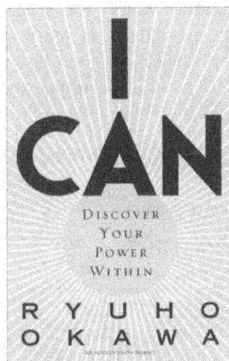

## I CAN

### DISCOVER YOUR POWER WITHIN

Paperback • 103 pages • $14.95
ISBN: 978-1-937673-25-3

There are countless books on self-development, but none as deep and religious as I Can -Discover Your Power Within- by Ryuho Okawa. In this enlightening masterpiece by Okawa, the Master and CEO of Happy Science, you can gain stronger confidence in yourself, overcome adversities and anxieties, and make your dreams come true by learning the spirit of self-help and by knowing the secret to your creative power within.

*For a complete list of books, visit okawabooks.com*

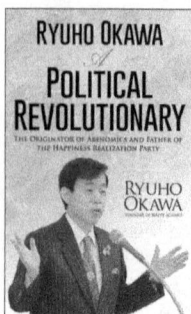

## RYUHO OKAWA
## A POLITICAL REVOLUTIONARY
### THE ORIGINATOR OF ABENOMICS AND FATHER OF THE HAPPINESS REALIZATION PARTY

Paperback • 152 pages • $14.95

ISBN: 978-1-941779-10-1

In this book, the Founder of Happy Science Group as well as the Father of Happiness Realization Party, Okawa lays down the guiding principles and the ways to breakthrough on the topics of economy, finance, nuclear power plant, foreign diplomacy, social welfare, and society with aging population and a falling birth rate.

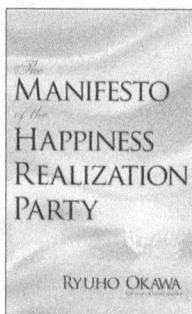

## THE MANIFESTO OF THE HAPPINESS REALIZATION PARTY

Paperback • 84 pages • $9.99

ISBN:978-1-937673-97-0

This book is a historical declaration to change the world through a peaceful revolution by the philosophy and speech based on the Truth, rather than by violence or massacre. It also states on the assessment of the meaning of WWII as well as how the relation between religion and politics should be. It is a must read for all people who wish to build a true utopia.

## INTO THE STORM OF INTERNATIONAL POLITICS
### THE NEW STANDARDS OF THE WORLD ORDER

Paperback • 154 pages • $14.95

ISBN:978-1-941779-27-9

The world is now seeking a new idea or a new philosophy that will show the countries with such values the direction they should head in. In this book, Okawa presents new standards of the world order while giving his own analysis on world affairs concerning the U.S., China, Islamic State and others.

*For a complete list of books, visit okawabooks.com*

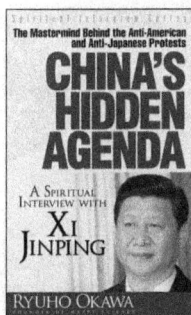

## China's Hidden Agenda

### The Mastermind Behind the Anti-American and Anti-Japanese Protests

Paperback • 182 pages • $14.95
ISBN:978-1-937673-18-5

"I wanted to stir up the anti-American movement in the Arab world to make sure that the United States won't be able to attack Syria or Iran...I'm the master-mind behind the Muhammad video."

—Xi Jinping's Guardian Spirit

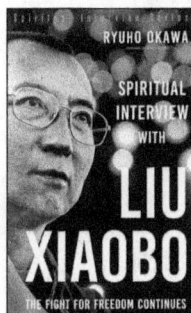

## Spiritual Interview with Liu Xiaobo

### The Fight for Freedom Continues

Paperback • 128 pages • $9.95
ISBN:978-1-943869-25-1

On July 21, 2017, 8 days after his death, the spirit of Liu Xiaobo was resurrected to deliver his messages. This book reveals the truths about China, a totalitarian country that doesn't grant freedom to its people. In this book, the Chinese Nobel Prize winner shares his wish to hand down the movement of China's democratization to future generations.

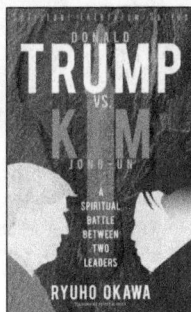

## Donald Trump vs. Kim Jong-un

### A Spiritual Battle between Two Leaders

Paperback • 170 pages • $9.95
ISBN:978-1-943869-27-5

Who will pull the trigger first, Kim Jong-un or Donald Trump? The North Korean issue is entering the final phase. This book tells Kim Jong-un's scenario and the crucial points of Donald Trump's strategy. Here is the top-secret information to the North Korean issue.

---

*For a complete list of books, visit okawabooks.com*

## Spiritual Interview with the Guardian Spirit of Joshua Wong

### His resolve to protect the freedom of Hong Kong

Paperback • 82 pages • $9.95
ISBN:978-1-943869-54-1

To those around the world who believe in God and pray for God's justice to be served, we hereby bring you the words of the guardian spirit of Joshua Wong Let there be glory in his courage and the freedom of Hong Kong.

## Spiritual Messages from Oscar Wilde

### Love, Beauty, and LGBT

Paperback • 80 pages • $9.95
ISBN:978-1-943869-50-3

Why did Oscar Wilde write the Happy Prince?

The Astonishing Truth:
- His spiritual connection to Jesus Christ
- The deeper meaning behind his homosexuality
- Advice for the LGBT people to become happy

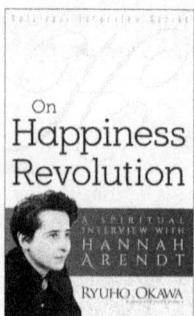

## On Happiness Revolution

### A Spiritual Interview with Hannah Arendt

Paperback • 134 pages • $14.95
ISBN:978-1-937673-82-6

This spiritual interview dives into the opinions of the German-Jewish political scientist and philosopher, Hannah Arendt. This book touches upon political phenomena, gives advice about political movements, and explains the importance of understanding God's love and justice.

---

*For a complete list of books, visit <u>okawabooks.com</u>*

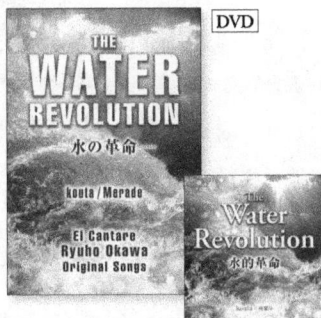

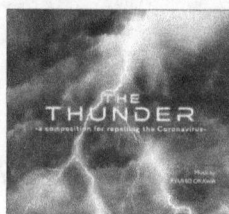